QUOTES FROM HERO LEADERS

"To love what you do and feel that it matters. How could anything be more fun?"
—KATHARINE GRAHAM

"Do not wait; the time will never be 'just right.' Start where you stand, and work with whatever tools you may have at your command, and better tools will be found as you go along."
—NAPOLEON HILL

"The most difficult thing is the decision to act, the rest is merely tenacity."
—AMELIA EARHART

"Happiness will never come if it's a goal in itself; happiness is a by-product of a commitment to worthy causes."
—NORMAN VINCENT PEALE

"Flaming enthusiasm, backed up by horse sense and persistence, is the quality that most frequently makes for success."
—DALE CARNEGIE

THE
HERO
FACTOR

HOW GREAT LEADERS
TRANSFORM ORGANIZATIONS
AND CREATE
WINNING CULTURES

JEFFREY W. HAYZLETT
WITH JIM EBER

Entrepreneur Press®

Entrepreneur Press, Publisher
Cover Design: Andrew Welyczko
Production and Composition: Eliot House Productions

This publication is designed to provide accurate and authoritative information
in regard to the subject matter covered. It is sold with the understanding that
the publisher is not engaged in rendering legal, accounting or other professional
services. If legal advice or other expert assistance is required, the services of a
competent professional person should be sought.

Entrepreneur Press® is a registered trademark of Entrepreneur Media, Inc.

Library of Congress Cataloging-in-Publication Data
    Names: Hayzlett, Jeffrey W.
    Title: The hero factor: how great leaders transform organizations and create
       winning cultures / by Jeffrey W. Hayzlett with Jim Eber.
    Description: Irvine, California: Entrepreneur Media, Inc., [2018] | Includes
       bibliographical references.
    Identifiers: LCCN 2018032608 | ISBN 978-1-64201-131-9 |
       ISBN 1-64201-131-2
    LC record available at https://lccn.loc.gov/2018032608

Printed in the United States of America

22 21 20 19 18   10 9 8 7 6 5 4 3 2 1

To the hero business leaders who have led the way to build their communities, enrich the lives of others, and make this world a better place. And to the future heroes who are inspired to follow in those leaders' footsteps to build new hero cultures, teams, and businesses and leave this world better than the way they found it.

CONTENTS

ORIGIN STORY

By many key indicators, the American economy was on fire in 1998. Unemployment was the lowest it had been in 30 years. Wages were on the rise for many workers. America was growing, and I was one of the beneficiaries of that growth. I had already made my first million and my businesses were doing well. I had a happy life and a great family, but I still had regular throwdowns with my father-in-law, Bob, on our favorite subjects: politics and business.

Bob has been a hardworking farmer all his life. He will ride a tractor until we pry his cold, dead hands off it—and he shows no signs of letting go. All our conversations have been fun, but few have stuck in my mind like the one we had in fall 1998.

I didn't think there was much to debate, but there we were, talking about the state of American business, when Bob looked directly at me and made a comment about the "fat cats"—the people taking in millions of dollars—and how they don't pay their fair share.

Anyone who knows me knows it takes the metaphorical equivalent of a truck hitting me to render me speechless, even for a moment. But there I was, unable to speak as I processed what Bob had said. "Who do you think those fat cats are?" I finally asked him. "By your definition, *I'm* one of those fat cats. Do you think I don't pay my fair share?"

Bob shook his head no, but I wasn't convinced. So I hit him with all I had: "Right. I'm your son-in-law, and I pay my fair share. Most of the people you call 'fat cats' who I know do, too. What you're saying is based on the perception of a few. Most of the richest Americans do great things. Taking them down doesn't build us up; it destroys the people who work for them."

Bob seemed like he wanted to respond, but I was on a roll. "To say the richest people are evil simply because they make money also ignores that capitalism creates altruism. You can only win in capitalism by providing a service or selling something people need or want. Most of these people you call 'fat cats' simply found a way to do that by building, creating, or innovating and making this country great. Nothing works in America without paying for it in some way, and someone is going to profit from that. To say rich people don't pay their share ignores their contributions to the process of human advancement."

I'll be honest: I don't remember what Bob said next. But after I got down from my soapbox, I understood why he said what he said: Perception is reality. I could see just how corrupt the idea of anyone making millions like those "fat cats" was from his point of view: For them to win, everyone else had to lose, especially people like Bob, who work hard and get their hands dirty. Some of the things he saw in 1998 still resonate with people today: inflated CEO salaries backed by golden parachutes no matter how badly they fail; well-paying jobs being sent overseas to improve margins and enrich shareholders; hardworking families and farmers like Bob getting squeezed for every dollar and foreclosed on by "heartless" banks; the worship of Wall Street over Main Street. The list goes on. But most of the "fat cats" I knew personally were making money legally and respectably. They might not literally get their hands dirty working the land to earn a living like my father-in-law, but what they did was not dirty. I was convinced Bob was only seeing the bad side of business.

Now, if you're expecting a "come-to-Jesus" moment, where Bob opens my eyes to the truth and I hear my call to hero leadership, you're as wrong as he was. He may have been a farmer not far from Iowa, but this was not my *Field of Dreams* moment.

At the time, I didn't question whether there was more than just perception to Bob's reality, but there was. I didn't see that while the economy was growing, wages stayed stagnant for many Americans. I didn't make the connection that while productivity was increasing, people were working hundreds of hours more for less pay. That income inequality was still on the rise. That the richest 10 percent were reaping almost all the benefits of growth. America was growing, but not everyone was winning. In fact, fewer and fewer were. Then the dotcom bubble burst at the dawn of the 21st century, and America learned that some of those gains were nothing but air.

But I didn't see any of that at the time. I was doing well, and I knew I was doing right by my family, the people who worked for me, and myself. How could I be wrong if I was sure what I was doing was right?

I'll be honest again: Even when I got that first call to hero leadership, more than a decade later as America struggled to recover from the Great Recession, I didn't answer it. Because, again, I didn't feel I was doing anything wrong, and truthfully, I wasn't. I was doing well, and I didn't feel I needed to do more. And doing well is good. It's fine.

But it's not being a hero.

THE CALL TO HERO LEADERSHIP AND THE HERO FACTOR

As you read this book, you'll find that hero leadership is a choice—a choice to be more than good, more than great, no matter the circumstances. Hero leadership does not choose you. It is a conscious choice leaders and companies make: to decide what they value and to *hold themselves accountable* to live those values consistently and sustainably in everything they do. This is where our Hero Factor journey begins. In this first part, I'll walk you through what that call to leadership might look like for you (every origin story is different, after all). Then we'll create a working definition of your Hero Factor and learn how you can measure it.

Let's go.

CHAPTER 1

THE CALL TO HERO LEADERSHIP

Meet Bubba. Things aren't going so well for him, until one day he passes a billboard for the lottery and sees it's at a record jackpot. If he could only win the lottery, he thinks, that would solve all his problems.

So Bubba gets down on his knees and prays: "Lord, please let me win the lottery; please let me win the lottery; please let me win the lottery . . ."

Every day, Bubba gets down on his knees and prays. He also makes sure to live his best life. He does good deeds. He goes to church. He tells everyone that God will provide. He knows it! He feels it! But when Saturday's drawing comes, Bubba doesn't win. Next week, the same thing. And the following week. And the following week. Week after week, the jackpot grows, but Bubba never wins.

Finally, someone else claims that record prize. Upon hearing the news, Bubba finally breaks down, falls to his knees, and cries out, "God, why didn't I win? I've been a good soul and a good citizen. I've prayed and gone to church. I felt you would provide. Why?"

And to Bubba's surprise, the Lord answers him.

"Bubba, you got to buy a ticket."

Not even God can help you if you don't make the choice that leads to what you want. Hearing the call is one thing. Choosing to answer it is another.

But this is not a book about God. Or the lottery. But it is about Bubba, in a way. Because in a book about hearing and answering the call to hero leadership, I'm not just starting with a joke about Bubba. *I am Bubba.* Or at least I started out that way. I literally took a call to hero leadership and then refused to buy my ticket.

In 2009, Randy Garn, a founding partner of Hero Partners, invited me to attend their annual meeting in Jackson Hole, Wyoming. Hero Partners was a nationwide invitation-only entrepreneurs' club for leaders from fast-growth companies who pledge themselves to hero leadership and who collaborate to revive the spirit of American entrepreneurialism. These were people and companies I knew and/or admired. It was an honor to be considered as a guest, let alone be invited to join. Randy and the other members must have seen something in me that aligned with their vision of Hero Partners' future.

So of course, I said *no.* (Just call me Bubba.)

In all fairness, the future was uncertain for me and the country at the time. As America struggled to recover from the Great Recession, I was entering what would be my final year at Kodak as its CMO. But the following year, I had left Kodak, and Randy called again. I still said no. Next year, the same thing. And the next year. One year he even put Rudy Ruettiger on the phone to help recruit me—*the* Rudy from Notre Dame, the guy who inspired the film *Rudy* (one of my all-time favorite sports movies). It was amazing to talk to him, but still . . . *nope.*

For seven years Randy called me, and for seven years I said, "No." *No. No. No. No. No. No. No.*

But the eighth time, I not only answered Randy's call to become a Hero Partner, but to borrow a legendary phrase from Victor Kiam, I loved it so much I bought the company. Well, part of it: The Hero Club, a nationwide organization of business leaders who pledge themselves to hero leadership. We have expanded well beyond Jackson Hole to host hundreds of leaders in cities across the country who genuinely care about leading and serving others. We unite to collaborate, communicate, and inspire hero leadership in one another and in and through our companies.

My work with The Hero Club inspired me to write this book, but it also forced me to reflect on why I resisted Randy's call for so long. I wasn't really Bubba. I made a conscious choice *not* to buy my ticket to Hero Partners. But I was seeking to understand what changed in me, so I could explain it to you and the other members of The Hero Club. Because I felt different. So different that I made it part of my business, not just how I do business. So why did I wait so many years to buy my ticket?

- ▼ Was it because committing to hero leadership is hard? No, I've never been afraid of hard work, and I know leading the right way requires grit, determination, and focus.
- ▼ Was it because I didn't have the time? Time is a precious commodity, but I make time for the things that are important to me.
- ▼ Was it because I didn't understand what it meant to be a hero leader? Maybe, but I had a good idea what it meant, and certainly respected Randy and the other people who attended.
- ▼ Was it because I didn't want to challenge the status quo? Come on, have you met me? I love a challenge as much as I like disrupting the status quo.

None of my "becauses" answered my "why." But as I started to write this book, I looked in the mirror and realized I still saw a Bubba who wasn't ready to be a hero, who didn't understand what it meant, and who didn't know why it was important. In other words, I still didn't think I was a hero.

Sure, I had what I thought were hero qualities. I demand authenticity from myself and those who work for me. I have always tried to be the best "me" I can be and encourage that in others. I am clear on what my values are and how they reflect the values of the company. I push to break free from antiquated leadership models. I strive to be an inclusive, strong, decisive yet open leader and to set a good example for my people and other leaders so I can earn their trust. I encourage people to be themselves, not another version of me. Heck, I've already written three books on business leadership in addition to leading businesses of all sizes.

But did all that add up to being a hero? The answer was no. I was a good—sometimes great—leader at a good—sometimes great—company, but a hero? I wanted to be one, but I wasn't there yet. I'm nowhere near perfect, and the idea of calling myself a hero was, at the very least, uncomfortable. I *wish* I was as good as the others with whom I have surrounded myself.

This revelation became a mirror moment for me—a kind of business confessional to myself. "You hypocritical son of a bitch," I said to my "reflection." How many times had I *not* done all those things I just said? Disappointed people? Disappointed myself? Done something unheroic when I knew better? Missed the point? Got stuck in the past? Ignored a problem I knew was happening? Failed to listen? Not made time for people or fully followed through on something? Failed to attain the operational success I wanted and needed? Walked around with what I call Johnny Vegas Syndrome like I knew better than everyone else?

These "mirror moments" of genuine vulnerability have a way of actually making you stronger. As I asked and answered this exhausting list of questions, I realized that I wasn't just ready to make that choice and invest in myself and The Hero Club. I was ready to explain why it mattered. I was ready to own it as part of my purpose—what Simon Sinek would call my "why."

And why was I doing this? Because I felt something changing, not just in me but in the country I love. I believe we are at a crossroads where we have a chance for real change in the way we do business. All those people looking for purpose and direction ask: Who will lead? Who will propel innovation, change the culture of the workplace to be more inclusive, and drive the evolution of this country?

The answer: the heroes.

> *Entrepreneurialism is America's spirit.*
> *Hero is America's destination.*

We need hero leaders and companies to reclaim the best parts of the American spirit of free enterprise and entrepreneurialism. We need to abandon the scarcity mentality (for me to win, you or someone else has to lose) for an abundance mentality that is win-win for all. But if we as a nation are going to do this, organizations and their leaders need to light a collective fire. And to start this fire, we need catalysts: more leaders and companies that are choosing the path of hero leadership. That's where we start: by making a choice.

IT'S TIME TO PICK A SIDE

I believe we are entering the age of hero businesses and leaders. This may sound strange in the era of #MeToo, when people we thought were our heroes are being exposed for decidedly unheroic acts and attitudes. But that's the point! Hero is a destination, one you choose to drive to and hold yourself accountable for once you get there. It's not a place you can automatically or accidentally end up—even if you win the lottery. We have had enough of leaders who beat each other down and fail to build futures for us, our children, and our children's children. Now is the time for hero leaders to transform their organizations and reclaim what has been lost or stuck in the status quo. The door is open for hero companies and leaders to build that better tomorrow.

Are you ready to answer that call to hero leadership?

I'm ready, and I'm putting my size and my mouth—and those of you who know me know that both are quite large—behind answering that call to hero leadership and helping you feel it so you answer it, too.

But first, let's talk about what exactly I mean by the word "hero." When I say "hero," for our purposes here I'm not talking about the first responders, police, firefighters, and the men and women of our military who put their lives on the line to protect ours. I'm also not talking about people who risk their lives to save someone else. God bless all of them, but no one needs to die to be a hero in corporate America. Besides, it takes much more than a single act of heroism to make a hero. You need to have the courage to light and run into the proverbial fire again and again. So if you think reading this book will do the trick, or cutting a big check to charity will turn you from a zero to a hero, I hope you saved your receipt.

I'm done with anyone who sees people as commodities—pawns to enrich themselves alone. Enough with the villains and predators, losers and louts, lazy asses and complacent cowards, pessimists and naysayers, obstructionists and clowns, blamers and dividers, politicians and PR people who say the right things but never act on them.

What I'm asking is for *you* to become a person with big ideas and noble ideals who preaches *and* puts into practice the principles of this book. Someone of spirit and tenacity, values and purpose, goodness and selflessness, who leads your organization or team from the head and the heart. I'm looking for social entrepreneurs and CEOs, business owners small and large who have the courage and commitment to consistently and constantly give back *and* give more to serve others— even when warning signs and Wall Street say to quit. The ones who welcome all people and all points of view to the table. The ones who make a difference in people's lives and still beat the competition to win in the workplace and marketplace.

Yes, you can win and have fun doing it, by serving people (and again I mean *all* people), partners, communities, customers, country, environment, *and* the bottom line at the same time.

Read that list carefully. Because those of you looking for an anti-capitalist, money-is-the-root-of-all-evil, one-percenters-must-go-down manifesto should also return this book now. Hero companies and leaders—whether they are solo practices or have millions of global employees—can do all the above without dismissing the power of profit. No one in this book will ask you to accept the notion that making money is wrong. Heroes in my book are not saviors, martyrs, or even saints. Some of them can be jackasses or deeply flawed—and some of them are reluctant heroes. I realize that hero leaders and companies aren't perfect and never will be. They're more like my favorite superheroes—not the gods or demigods like Thor and Wonder Woman or aliens like Superman, but troubled, conflicted capitalists with no special powers, who in "real life" run great companies or countries, like Batman, Black Panther, and Iron Man—especially Iron Man, as he doesn't hide who he is from the world.

Then again, don't think you need to have a fortune like Bruce Wayne or Tony Stark to be a hero leader. The Bill Gateses, Warren Buffetts, and Mark Zuckerbergs of the world may get the headlines and pledged to give their fortunes back in the long run, but America needs more everyday heroes, who are creating a better future built on the entrepreneurial roots that made this country great. One built on the foundation of the past but evolving to include more people in its progress. Some heroes might hail from Park Avenue, but I'm betting that many more live on Main Street.

These heroes understand a quote attributed to Henry Ford: "A business that makes nothing but money is a poor business." Money may be how we keep score, but any idiot can make money. We share this world with others and have a purpose beyond it. We need leaders and companies with hero mindsets who understand that. Without the right mindset, you'll never develop the qualities and implement the strategies to be a hero leader. You'll never have the highest Hero Factor.

But what does that mean, Jeff? Great question! I'm glad you asked!

THE HERO MINDSET

Having a hero mindset means today's leaders, entrepreneurs, and business owners know they can't just serve their clients, shareholders, and themselves and expect their employees to take the leftovers. They need to connect with, listen to, and include their people (as well as customers, clients, partners, vendors, and communities) in the conversations about the business. They must make them feel that their goals are aligned with the goals of the business and its leaders—because they are. *Because they have real values.* Not just on paper, in the words of their corporate mission statements and annual reports, but seen every day in the culture of the organization.

That's the first essential step in how companies and leaders display the Hero Factor. You may be on your way already. I believe most companies and leaders are, like me and my business, basically good. They *want* to be heroes. They just might not be as far along as they think in living, driving, and aligning their values through the organization. Or maybe they were doing well for a while but got stuck in their stories. They became heroes or got close and then got complacent and failed to consistently and sustainably invest in and listen to their customers and the market, and coach their people to:

▼ break free from the status quo and create and sustain hero cultures;

▼ serve others and the common good;

▼ avoid "reasons why not" and the lure of the dark side when things get tough; and

▼ strive to create the next generation of hero leaders.

That's what I realized about myself and what The Hero Club needed, too. Years before I joined, it only accepted CEOs and heads of billion-dollar companies. I argued that while operational excellence and sustained revenue were essential, you shouldn't need a pedigree worthy of Davos or Sun Valley to earn a Hero Club invite. We needed to welcome leaders whose fortunes did not equal the GDP of several countries combined, and whose corrupt corporate cultures often fail to value profits *and* people. We needed the next generation of heroes, who rarely grab headlines and run businesses built on more than advertising slogans and spin. Who find ways to lead with a greater purpose that goes beyond free coffee in the office. Who give back in ways beyond the well-meaning yet passive giving of a portion of proceeds going to charity. Who go beyond sharing their treasure and use their time and talent to make an impact all year long.

If that sounds like you, then let's take the ride to hero leadership together. Let's break free from antiquated leadership models, partisan politics, and valueless direction and create more hero leaders for our children and grandchildren's future.

Let's *choose* to be heroes.

WHAT IS YOUR HERO FACTOR?

The Hero Factor of any organization and leader is determined by combining scores from 0 to 10 on two equally weighted scales all heroes must hold themselves accountable to: Operational Excellence and Hero Intensity. Thus, the Hero Factor equation is as follows:

Operational Excellence (0–10) + Hero Intensity (0–10) = Your Hero Factor (0–20)

To get your Operational Excellence, Hero Intensity, and Hero Factor scores, take the Hero Factor Assessment at the end of this book or online by clicking the Hero Assessment link on the websites for The Hero Factor (https://HeroFactorBook.com), The Hero Club (https://heroceoclub.com/), or The Hayzlett Group (http://hayzlett.com/). Then plot them on the Hero Factor Scale (shown in Figure 1.1, on page 12) to see what type of hero you are (or aren't). Take it as many times as you want: See where you stand now, after you finish the rest of Part

---

WHAT IS YOUR HERO FACTOR?, continued

I (which defines all three parts of the equation), and after you finish the whole book (which goes into depth on both parts of your Hero Intensity and the heart of your Hero Factor: your values and how you value others). See if your assessment of your Hero Factor changes!

Figure 1.1 The Hero Factor Scale

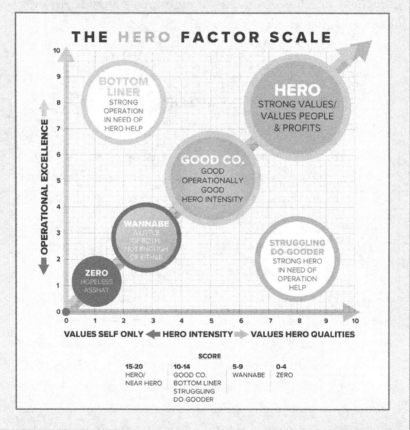

CHAPTER 2

OPERATIONAL EXCELLENCE

Most of you know what operational excellence means for what you do and how long you have been in business. You have also heard it discussed and dissected countless times by me and those much smarter than me in books, videos, blogs, magazines, TV shows, and elsewhere, which makes Operational Excellence the easier of the two scales to define and definitely the least messy part of the Hero Factor equation. So while I dedicate two parts of this book to understanding your and your organization's Hero Intensity (the heart of the Hero Factor), this short chapter is all the time I will spend on Operational Excellence (the head of the Hero Factor). That's not because Operational Excellence isn't essential—after all, it's half your Hero Factor score—but because it is so much simpler to define.

That said, Operational Excellence *will* live in the background (and occasionally the foreground) of all we discuss when it comes to your Hero Intensity; I simply will not go into much depth on it beyond this chapter and will spend little time defining terms any experienced businessperson should know. I couldn't possibly lay out the details, nuances, and exceptions that apply to every organization, industry, and customer base. Nor will I try. There are countless books (including my first three) that can help you understand what operational excellence means for the size and scale of your business and how to improve on micro and macro levels.

What I will do is provide this general definition of operational excellence for any and all organizations: *execution of a business strategy that leads to real, consistent, and reliable results that are measurable and sustainable, despite the risks and costs and even as your products and services change and evolve to meet marketplace demands.*

For most organizations big or small, this definition means executing on all these things over time:

▼ Products and/or services that exceed the competition and industry standards

▼ Real growth and increased revenues over time

▼ A broad, consistent, and connected set of customers/clients that you always focus on and create value for

▼ External partners that provide expertise, reach, and knowledge beyond what you know

▼ Profitability

▼ Reduced costs and efficiency

▼ Investment in people and productivity

▼ Productive workplaces (whether you are a business of one or have teams and offices around the globe) focused on that growth and serving those customers

▼ Willingness to take and mitigate risks—even when you take big ones

▼ Success through tough times small and big (either self-generated or brought upon you by forces beyond your control)

▼ Constantly attracting and recruiting talent

▼ Investment in and a plan for adding more value for the future through innovation, increased customer engagement, and new or improved products and services

I say above this list applies to "most organizations." While I find it hard to believe that a company has any hope of operational success, let alone excellence, if it lacks most or all of these things, it is possible that revenue and profitability are not as important in the short term for some businesses as, say, R&D or customer acquisition. But even if that is true, it can't last forever. For example, a pharmaceutical company spending millions on research won't survive if its drugs don't get FDA approval. Or consider Tesla. What it does may be really cool, but with losses of $5.4 billion and counting as of 2018, if it can't produce the cars it promised to scale, eventually customers will stop lining up—and so will its investors.

This leads me to another point about this list: doing them "over time."

EXCELLENCE TODAY IS NO GUARANTEE OF EXCELLENCE TOMORROW

Regardless of the size and scale of your company, operational excellence is something that changes every year—and must evolve faster than ever if you want to survive. I spent five years of my professional life at Kodak. I know what it is like to see an iconic brand struggle to reinvent and reimagine itself when the market for its products fades into history. Things can change—fast—for companies large and small, because time to market is exponentially quicker than it was a generation ago.

For example, according to growth strategy consulting firm Innosight, in 1964, companies spent an average of 33 years on the S&P 500. By 2016, it was 24 years. That's projected to drop to 12 years by 2027, which means half of the companies on the S&P 500 as I write this will be gone by then. Some of them will be acquired by bigger companies. Some will be done in by changing times, consumer tastes, and technologies. But many of them will be undone or forced to reinvent themselves by nimble, hungry, aggressive, disruptive, and smart small businesses and entrepreneurs that are growing fast and make up for what they lack in scale and infrastructure with innovation. They reinvent what is possible, taking on and taking down the status quo by thinking big and acting bigger. More than a few of these future S&P 500 companies probably don't exist as I write this. The creator of the next Facebook, Shake Shack, or Lyft could be staring at the clock in a high school or even middle school classroom right now, waiting for the bell to ring, the next big thing just a glimmer in their eyes.

Think of it this way: Who wore yoga pants a generation ago? According to the *Financial Times*, imports of yoga pants exceeded those of jeans in the United States in 2017, and those same pants and all leggings have been added to the goods that the United Kingdom uses to track inflation.

Of course, the odds of operational excellence and success over time for those new and existing small businesses and entrepreneurs are pretty steep too, especially in the early years. Fail at one or two things on that list for even a few months, let alone a year, and things can get dicey. They can try to rationalize and convince themselves they just need this or that to happen to succeed, but the fact is most small businesses will fail. Of course, as we all know, failure is often part of the foundation for future success. But once they succeed, those companies can't relax: They need to continue to adapt, transform, and innovate to find new sources of revenue—even as they maintain existing ones—lest they be taken down by a business that sees new and different opportunities.

OPERATIONAL EXCELLENCE DOES NOT EQUAL HERO

While operational excellence usually means making money immediately and over time at the highest level and having a bottom line that is secure and growing, that alone won't make you a hero. Many of you undoubtedly noticed that the list defining operational excellence is a reasonably objective measurement of operational standards. Operational Excellence is *Dragnet*'s Joe Friday of the Hero Factor: *Just the facts, ma'am.*

This is why I said Operational Excellence is the easier of the two Hero Factor scales to define, and maybe even a little boring to discuss. *But not to do.* Making money is almost always exciting, and if that bores or bothers you, maybe think about giving this book to someone else.

Granted, it used to be that making money by producing great products and offering valuable services was the sole measurement of operational excellence and American greatness. In some ways, it still is: The legendary Fortune 500 list was a child of this belief. The list first appeared in 1955 and since then has ranked public and private companies with publicly available data in the U.S. by just one measurement: revenue. Of course, the nature of that revenue and what generates it has changed. In line with what I said above about the S&P 500, it is worth noting that only 60 of the original 500 companies listed in 1955—including Boeing, GM, Procter & Gamble, and IBM—were still on the list in 2017.

Revenue remains an absolutely vital part of what makes a company great, but it's a much smaller part of what determines a company and its leaders' Hero Factor. And this is where things get harder to define. The reason the operational excellence list is so simple and straightforward is what's *not* on it: anything to do with values, people, culture, inclusiveness, and giving back. In other words, the human side of the equation. The people side. The *hero* side of your Hero Factor: the Hero Intensity.

The reason I separated out Hero Intensity is you *can* have Operational Excellence without it. As I said before, companies and Wall Street have for generations used revenue, the bottom line, and profits as *the* barometer for greatness. Some of those "fat cats" my father-in-law was talking about surely did. Does that make them evil? No. You still need revenue, and sometimes you have to focus on it when you must make hard decisions in order to survive. But you need to balance that excellence against the things people usually group under "soft skills," when really they are nothing but hard. Hard to do, hard to sustain, and hard to measure. So they are the ones that get tested, not only when times are tough but also when times are good!

The question is: How do you truly live your Hero Intensity without compromising that excellence—and can you even enhance it? To answer that, we need to first understand what it is.

CHAPTER 3

HERO INTENSITY

*D*o *you value people over profit?*

That's often the first question I ask leaders about themselves and their companies to determine their Hero Intensity. What was your answer? If it was either "yes" or "no," chances are you're not a hero company or leader, because your Operational Excellence and Hero Intensity are out of balance. If you recall the Hero Factor Scale from Chapter 1, the answer is not profit over people or people over profit, but profit *and* people. Operational Excellence is the profit side and Hero Intensity is the "people" side, and that Hero Intensity is based on two factors:

▼ Your organization's and your values and how you live them
▼ How your organization and you value "others"—people and groups inside and outside the organization, the community, and the world we live in

Let's take a deeper dive into these two points.

YOUR VALUES

Everything—from your vision of where you want the company to go to how you treat your people and customers to the culture of your organization—flows from your values. This goes beyond what Simon Sinek might call your "why" or your purpose; they are your who, what, and how, too. Your values are the foundation for all you do at your company, and they state in no uncertain terms what you genuinely believe in.

> *Values must be lived, not just stated.*

This foundation starts with those values being clearly stated and tied to any mission statements. But those values must go beyond words. You must see and feel them in the actions of the people who work for you and communicate them to anyone who connects to or through you.

That said, ask yourself, your organization, your leadership, and all your people the following questions:

▼ Do you have your values clearly articulated?
▼ Are they written out for all to see?
▼ Can you and all your people, as well as your customers, partners, community, etc., see and say what they are?
▼ Do your people live those values? What's the evidence that you and they live them?
▼ Do they show up in the products you produce and/or services you offer?

▼ Do you review them regularly to ensure you are living them and they still support your direction as an organization?

▼ How firm are you in them? How have they changed and evolved?

We will consider these questions more deeply in the following chapters. But notice I did not ask what your values are—just that they be clearly stated. That's because what they are is irrelevant to determining your Hero Factor. Doing what's right is simply about choosing to be the best you can be for others in the service of your values, whatever they may be. Unless your values are illegal or directly or indirectly advocate hate or violence, I cannot and will not judge them in this book. I will force you to take a hard look at them and how they are being lived and driven through your organization and its leadership. But my only judgment even then will be whether you have them, know what they are, and honor them.

Now that doesn't mean I cannot judge those values as a customer, potential partner, or citizen of my community. I am free to choose to support and do business with whom I please. But the more I reject people or businesses that offer the products or services I need because I don't like how they look or what they believe in favor of those who are not clearly living and articulating their values, the more I compromise who I am, what I am doing, and my own values. And that lowers my Hero Intensity and, thus, my Hero Factor.

The real problem is not when values clash with yours, but how many leaders out there can't actually say what they and their organizations truly value and then live those values consistently and sustainably in everything they do.

Can you? Do you know the immutable, indisputable things you and your business stand for? Could you show how they permeate your culture and how those values align with the mission of the company and what the company *says* it values? If not, you aren't a hero to anyone, let alone yourself and your business. That doesn't make you wrong, evil, or even a hypocrite. You might be a nice person and run a nice place to work. But it does lower your Hero Intensity.

I am reminded of the line from Matthew 7:1 in the New Testament: "Judge not, that ye be not judged." This is often interpreted as meaning "don't judge," which is a fine enough sentiment, but it is much deeper than that. It means you shouldn't judge unless you are willing to expose yourself to the same judgment. It means hold yourself to the same standard you demand of others. *It means don't be a damned hypocrite.* Heroes who live their values are rarely hypocrites, but when they are—and we all make mistakes— they are strong enough to admit they are wrong, rather than hide, cover it up, or offer halfhearted or inauthentic mea culpas. They take responsibility, and then hold themselves accountable for making sure it doesn't happen again.

That second part—accountability—is key. Apologies are useless without acknowledging and understanding the mistake and then actually holding yourself accountable for preventing them in the future. As I finish this book, any number of companies are facing mea culpa moments, including Facebook (fallout from the Cambridge Analytica revelations), Starbucks (calling the police to remove two African-American men from a store in Philadelphia), Uber (toxic culture and poor treatment of drivers), and Wells Fargo (fined millions of dollars for creating fake accounts). The question is, will those turn into mirror moments—hard looks at themselves that lead to actual changes in the way those companies operate—or are they just trying to placate us until the news cycle ends? The latter is a special kind of arrogance that undermines your Hero Intensity. Don't fall for it.

I'll cover this in more depth in Chapter 7, but for now know the real test of your Hero Intensity is what happens after a mistake is made or when the mistakes are discovered. Does it lead to real change in values and the way the business is run and how leadership conducts itself? Or will it just result in a proclamation of plans for change followed by little action once public scrutiny fades? How you take responsibility and hold yourself accountable determines how much forgiveness others have and how far your Hero Intensity falls. If companies are willing to reevaluate their values and beliefs, they can genuinely change how they act. Just like being strong enough to admit when you have failed to live by the values you promote, being willing to open yourself up to the possibility of changing them—and actually *doing* it—can raise your Hero Factor.

But, Jeff, doesn't that make me a hypocrite? It is *not* hypocritical to change and evolve your position, and thus what you value, if done in an authentic way. Anyone can make a bad choice. Anyone can be blinded by a little self-righteousness now and again. No one is perfect. Heroes are human, and all humans are flawed. The question is whether the flaw derives from a series of bad choices and mistakes that hurt others or a single bad decision or moment of weakness. The beliefs you had about people or organizations being heroes can certainly be undone by revelations about those mistakes (#MeToo is a good example).

As we will cover in Chapter 9, it is entirely human to reconsider our opinions as we learn what we don't know and connect with others who force us to challenge the power of our convictions. What does make you a hypocrite is attacking others' values when you cannot clearly state your own, or doing it to take down a competitor or win a job, a vote, a sale, donations, etc.—or in desperation to survive.

> *One heroic act does not make a hero or undo bad acts.*
> *Even Bernie Madoff gave money to charity.*

We need businesses and their people to lead the way in the age of heroes, and it starts with their values—whatever they are—and respecting those who have and live them. This nation was built on freedom of expression, free enterprise, and accepting and bridging differences in order to prosper. That means accepting that people will believe differently and live their lives very differently than I do. That means, as I said earlier, accepting that businesses that offer products and services I need may choose to support causes that go against my beliefs. I should not just accept that but value it as an American.

The true test of your values is having and living them—understanding what those values are, which ones are absolute, and which ones can evolve as you grow, listen to, and value others.

That brings us to the second part of determining your Hero Intensity.

HOW YOU VALUE OTHERS

When I say "others" in this book, I mean the people who connect to you and your business: the people who work with and for you, your customers and clients, your vendors and partners, your community, and even the environment.

Your Hero Intensity when it comes to valuing others can be found most broadly by looking at three things:

Culture

More than people living the values of the company and more than the mood of the organization, culture is the *feel* of the organization—or, more correctly, how its people make it feel, both individually and in teams. People are your greatest asset—strengths to be cultivated, not made to conform. There's a great management mantra that goes something like: "My job as a manager is to coach you to succeed and grow in your job." Great leaders don't work alone, and they don't claim all the glory for themselves. This requires skills many leaders find difficult to master:

- ▼ Allowing your people the entrepreneurial independence to pursue and grow opportunities and possibilities while still demanding results
- ▼ Aligning the values of the people who work for you with the values of the company so they share common goals
- ▼ Listening—really listening—to your people and admitting when you're wrong to create an environment of trust built on real relationships
- ▼ Creating transparency by being open, honest, and vulnerable
- ▼ Being decisive yet grounded by maintaining confidence through the chaos and uncertainty

Inclusivity

The Hero Factor is about all people, not just people like you. That means bringing *everyone*—all kinds of people and their different perspectives—to the proverbial table and allowing them to impact decisions, directions, and growth. Hero companies always have time for diversity but not drama or distraction. (Yes, boomers and beyond, that means Millennials, as well as the other identifiers that divide us, like gender, race, ethnicity, sexuality, political and religious beliefs, and so on.)

Giving Back and More

How do you give back to your people, your community, and beyond? Ask yourself these questions:

- ▼ How is the giving measured and directed?
- ▼ Does it go beyond dollars?
- ▼ How do you empower others in your organization to do and give more?
- ▼ What will be the legacy you leave behind? What lasting impact will you have?

Just like with Operational Excellence, there will be exceptions to everything I say above. For example, you may work in a local or national government agency or face hiring rules that give you less flexibility on how you can adjust the culture.

You may face strict protocols that exist for the safety of your people and others that mandate absolute precision in the way certain tasks are performed. But are your people smiling while they perform those jobs? With a few cultural and other exceptions, like the Queen's Guard at Buckingham Palace, most people don't smile because they don't want to—not because they are not allowed.

In the end, make sure you aren't using what you *can't* do as an excuse for not doing anything else. You need to challenge the way things have always been done, and you need to do it more than once. Anyone can do something once. You can jump out of a plane without a parachute once. One act of kindness or generosity does not move the needle from zero to hero. It takes hundreds or even thousands of values-driven, unselfish, unrecognized, often small acts every day—acts that are the foundation for the legacy you want to leave behind.

But don't assume that legacy is a given. Heroes aren't just made in a moment, and they're not assured of staying heroes once they get there. Your Hero Factor index is not static. You need to keep coming back to this again, and again, and again, to ask yourself, "Do I still have the Hero Factor?" But I'm getting ahead of myself. The rest of this book examines all the parts of your Hero Intensity and how to raise and maintain it. Before we begin, however, it helps to know where you are starting from and how it all adds up to determine your Hero Factor.

CHAPTER 4

YOUR **HERO** FACTOR

Now that you have what you need to evaluate your Operational Excellence and a basic understanding of your Hero Intensity, let's go back to the Hero Factor equation at the end of Chapter 1:

Operational Excellence (0–10) + Hero Intensity (0–10) =
Your Hero Factor (0–20)

Since Operational Excellence and Hero Intensity are weighted equally, a simple bit of addition will tell you where you fall on the Hero Factor scale. Whether you work on Main Street or are traded publicly on Wall Street, the scale is the same. Your Hero Factor isn't about your ability to make millions or billions; it's about your Operational Excellence and Hero Intensity for the size you are or want to be. The lower your total, the lower your Hero Factor, and we have names for those types. From low to high:

- ▼ Zeroes are 0–4.
- ▼ Wannabes are 5–9.
- ▼ Good Cos. are 10–14.
- ▼ Heroes or Near Heroes are 15 or higher.

Sounds simple enough, right? These types should be fairly self-explanatory based on what I have covered so far. But you know there has to be a "but," and there is: Those four categories are for people and organizations that have balanced scores, little more than a difference of 2 between their Operational Excellence and Hero Intensity scores. In other words, a 5 in each category would score a 10 total and just fall into the Good Co. range, and so would a company that had a 6/4 split. But a company with a split of 7/3 in one direction or the other, despite also scoring a 10, falls out of the Good Co. orbit and into the orbit of one of the other two categories on the scale:

- ▼ Bottom Liners (high Operational Excellence, low or no Hero Intensity)
- ▼ Struggling Do-Gooders (low or no Operational Excellence, high Hero Intensity)

Let's look a little closer at all six of these categories before the deeper dive into Hero Intensity.

HERO

When organizations and their leaders have a high Hero Factor, they are more than just great places to work; most days their people can't wait to go to sleep so they can get up and get back to work the next day. Hero businesses, leaders, and cultures are constantly doing things for the right reasons and balance profit with people. They have an abundance or win-win mentality and pride themselves on their balance between their Operational Excellence and Hero Intensity—and hold themselves accountable to both simultaneously.

You see that balance everywhere you look, right down to the smallest details—it extends from leadership down throughout the company. It informs everything its leaders and, in turn, its people do. Rob Beyer, president and CEO of EarthBend, a telephony and IT solutions company, gave me an example I love: "I started this 20 years ago when I was a corporate guy, as a 'WWID'—What Would I Do? So the people who work for me get a chance to ask, 'What would I do if I was Rob, the CEO?' And there are no restrictions or boundaries. They get to put a presentation together, and the information that comes out of that is very powerful. Then they embrace it. They're part of it. There's buy-in. But then we also have a culture where you hold people accountable to those things. We use a phrase: 'Six Ps: Proper Preparation Prevents Piss-Poor Performance. If you come to a meeting and you're not prepared, we ask you to leave or we stop the meeting. I think a hero company embraces all sides of those traits."

But at Hero companies, it isn't just everyone who works for them who feels this balance; customers, partners, vendors, and communities feel it too. Big or small, they are entrepreneurial beacons of light in America's free enterprise system. They have a passion and a mission to be and deliver the best. They have predictable, measurable, and constant behavior and growth and push to innovate in order to adapt and grow more.

Hero companies and leaders challenge the status quo even when it's uncomfortable—even when they are doing well and must disrupt the way they have done business for a generation or more. However, just because a company is disruptive, challenges established business models, and remakes industries doesn't make them a Hero. There are many things about Amazon, Apple, Facebook, and Uber—to name a few companies often labeled disruptive—that make them unheroic in the way they treat their people, customers, partners, and others.

GOOD CO.: GOOD OPERATIONALLY AND GOOD HERO INTENSITY

I believe most businesses are good, both in terms of how they treat their people and their operations, so this is where I believe most companies live: Good Co., short for Good Company. These companies do many of the things Hero companies and leaders do, just not as intensely. And that's OK. It's OK to be good. I celebrate you. Holding at or above a five in Operational Excellence and Hero Intensity means you have the potential to be a Hero. But this is where the rubber meets the road. If you're in this category, you have a choice to make: Do you want more, or do you just want to keep from falling into the Wannabe category?

WANNABE: A LITTLE OPERATIONAL EXCELLENCE, A LITTLE HERO INTENSITY, NOT ENOUGH OF EITHER

Wannabes are exactly what they sound like: They *want to be* better operationally, they *want to have* a higher Hero Intensity, they *want to do and be* so many things . . . but they just aren't. It's all aspirational. But what they aren't and don't want to be is Zeroes. The vast majority of Wannabes are neither Zeroes on the rise nor so hopeless that they run the risk of becoming a Zero. They do, however, run the risk of going out of business, because they can't execute operationally or heroically. Many businesses that fail go out swinging as Wannabes. If you're a Wannabe, you are going to have to take a hard look at everything you do.

ZERO: HOPELESS ASSHAT

Zeroes are the lowest of the low. They never get it, never will, and never wanted to in the first place. The sole goal of a Zero is self-enrichment and enriching those close to them. Think Bernie Madoff and other Ponzi schemers. Think Gordon Gekko from *Wall Street*, who believes "greed is good." Think Martin Shkreli, who raised the price on the drug Daraprim by 56 times when he bought the company. Think David Brandon, former CEO of Toys "R" Us, asking for his $6.5 million bonus as the company filed for bankruptcy, while employees who worked in the stores and stayed loyal until the doors shut for good got no severance. I could go on, but I won't. I feel dirty just talking about those Zeroes. I want to focus on making more hero leaders and companies, not give these hopeless asshats any more space. I just need to take a shower first.

BOTTOM LINER: STRONG OPERATION IN NEED OF HERO HELP

If the only value that defines your success as a company is the bottom line, you're a Bottom Liner—a hero only to the bottom line. Does this make your organization, leadership, and shareholders evil? *Absolutely not.* Bottom Liner is not a negative term, like "Bottom Feeder." Bottom Liners are just not Heroes, because all they have is Operational Excellence, not Hero Intensity. For example, in 2018, Disney announced it was tying its employees' payouts from the tax cut to a promise not to unionize. Is that *wrong*? No. It's a business decision. But it sure as hell isn't a heroic one.

Many, many Americans have built their futures at companies like Disney making decisions just like that. Sure, I want to see more Bottom Liners become Good Cos. and Heroes, but I will defend their right to choose profit (Operational Excellence) over people (Hero Intensity) as long as they do it legally and don't harm others. In other words, profits, in general, raise your Operational Excellence score. All the things people mistakenly associate with Bottom Liners, like greed, self-enrichment, unsafe workplaces, destruction of the environment, and inflated CEO salaries, lower your Operational Excellence score.

So those of you complaining about the cost of movie candy and popcorn or the fact that L.L.Bean will no longer take returns of the 30-year-old jeans you bought at Goodwill for $1, no questions asked? That's not necessarily a Hero or a Zero. It's a company looking to make more money on the product they sell and survive, not screw you.

To that end, Bottom Liners with no Hero Intensity do have a scarcity or win-lose mentality (for me to win you have to lose—or for the bottom line to win, consumers or employees have to lose), but that's not illegal, immoral, or unethical. It's just not heroic. It prioritizes profit over people. So the question isn't, "What is a Bottom Liner doing wrong?" but "How long can a Bottom Liner maintain its

Operational Excellence before being challenged by a company that has Hero Intensity?"

Take GE, which was dropped from the Dow Jones Industrial Average in 2018 after a 110-year run. GE was a great company that had Operational Excellence but kind of lost its way as it expanded into all kinds of businesses like TV in order to grow. Today, as part of its turnaround plan, GE is scaling back to focus on its core businesses and moved and remade its headquarters to look more like the high-tech companies they compete against. But does anyone think GE is not looking at their bottom line first as they lay off tens of thousands of employees? Whatever they do to take care of their employees, it's because they have to, not because it is part of their core values. This applies to any Bottom Liner, not just GE.

Bottom Liners never think to stay up all night like Christine Ehrich, CEO of Industrial Solutions Network, a workers' comp physical therapy network, who lost 20 percent of her business when a client went in a different direction: "One of the non-negotiables I have is if at all possible, we don't let someone go," she says. "And I go to great lengths to figure out how to make that business up. How to maximize profitability. Whatever we need to do to not have that happen. We ended up coming up with a creative strategy to make up that 20 percent of the business and ended up getting referrals from our clinics that were in the network. We got really strategic and really creative and we found a way. And so I think my employees really recognize the leadership and that commitment to them that they have security in their jobs and that they have that trust level."

Bottom Liners never fire customers even if their values are misaligned, like Tom Landry, president and cofounder of Allegiance Staffing, a multistate industrial staffing specialist, did: "We walked away from a 13-year relationship with Igloo coolers because what they wanted us to do didn't match who we were as a company," he says. "And yeah, it was a lot of business and it was money and we just said, 'We're not going to compromise the company for one customer.' And I'm sorry, but there are a lot of people that'll do that."

Bottom Liners never value—let alone listen—to others much; unlike John Greco, who has made a point of valuing and listening to others in his long business career, breaking down silos in the process, most recently as CEO of integrated solutions provider to both for-profit and nonprofit segments Greco Associates: "Whether it's anyone in the organization or a supplier, a partner, a business partner, first try to understand what's important to the other person or the other organization, what they need, and what they're trying to achieve," he says. "If you can put yourself in their shoes, if you can engage in active listening, the organization is more likely to succeed. I saw that play out at AT&T Bell Labs, where we took hundreds of various academics and Ph.D.s in their individual disciplines and brought them together in the Consumer Lab. We wound up winning a Malcolm Baldrige Quality Award because they worked together instead of individually."

In the end, Bottom Liners can do the things Christine, Tom, John, and others like them do to develop their Hero Intensity while still getting results, which is essential. A company with high Hero Intensity won't be able to take a fat (or skinny) cat down if they lack Operational Excellence.

STRUGGLING DO-GOODER: HIGH HERO INTENSITY, LOW OR NO OPERATIONAL EXCELLENCE

In the cowboy world, we would call Struggling Do-Gooders "all hat, no cattle." They are martyrs, slaves, and worshipers of their hero cause but have nothing but their dedication to give. That's because they gave everything else away—or never had it to begin with. I love seeing those people on *Shark Tank* talking about how they will give away all this money to charity and be so good to their people as part of their business models—but lack any business to go with those models.

How many people can you actually help that way and for how long if you live below the bottom line? How many people are you going to help if no one wants what you're selling?

Most of us cannot survive on altruism. If you want to make life a win-win for everybody, you need some Operational Excellence. Heck, even if he didn't sell it, Jesus created a product that others wanted: He turned water into wine. If, like Jesus, you think serving the people you are responsible for means metaphorically washing their feet instead of coaching them? Well, you've got one of the worst hero complexes you can have: the savior complex. Your job as a hero business and leader is not to save others. You are not a white knight. You are not a god or a superhero. (Listen to Edna Mode from *The Incredibles* movie: "No capes!")

But like Jesus—if you really do have a product or service that can sell—you can come back. But only if you start taking the steps toward the operational excellence you need. In my first three books (*The Mirror Test, Running the Gauntlet,* and *Think Big, Act Bigger*), I lay out many ways to do this, so I won't recount them all here, but among the things to consider:

- ▼ Fire your time- and bottom-line-sucking customers. If they are taking up a disproportionate amount of time or costing you more than they are worth, it's time to say, "We love you, but we're going to miss you."
- ▼ Fire or at least reconsider your people—ALL your people, especially those who have been with you for a long time. Make sure they are still contributing excellence.
- ▼ Fire yourself from the things you don't do well but keep doing out of pride or ignorance.
- ▼ Charge what your products and services are worth: Overpricing is one thing, but selling for less than they are worth—or cost—is never going to lead to operational excellence.
- ▼ Find a way to give back more than money. Your personal time and product/service are easier to absorb on the bottom line than writing a check—and sometimes just as valuable. Make the donation part of profits, but make giving back about more than dollars.

It is worth noting that when I presented the Struggling Do-Gooder category to some leaders as I wrote this book, a few called it the "granola" category, meaning it was "crunchy." Like the '60s, man. But this is more image than reality. Communal living still requires operational excellence to survive. And some of the hippiest-dippiest people I have met (thanks, George Carlin) still want to make money; they just have a different end in mind for the means. My co-writer, Jim, told me about a guy, Mott Green, who before his untimely accidental death in 2013 ran the Grenada Chocolate Company as a completely egalitarian island cooperative: no one, top to bottom, made more than anyone else. Everyone shared in the wealth and achieved the same self-sufficiency.

But shared wealth was still the goal, not shared struggle. Grenada Chocolate may not have had all the operational excellence it wanted, but it was no Struggling Do-Gooder. It was making money and proud of it.

That said, Struggling Do-Gooders are *not* nonprofits. Nonprofits are like any other organization, and can fall in or around any of the six categories. For a nonprofit to be a Struggling Do-Gooder, it would have to give away the vast majority of its revenue to the people it is designed to help but fail to generate much revenue in the first place. But those nonprofits that have high operational success and give most of it away are not necessarily Heroes. They may give a lot back to help people outside their offices, but if the organization lacks internal values and has a toxic workplace? Then they can be Bottom Liners, Good Cos., or even Wannabes. And if nonprofits generate revenue but spend all of it on salaries and not the people they are supposed to help? Well, that's a total Zero—among the worst kind of asshats I know: They make money for themselves by pretending to help others. (Do your due diligence, people. Some "charities" give less than 10 percent of the money you donate to the people you thought they were helping.)

If you are a Struggling Do-Gooder, you can raise your Operational Excellence. But like Bottom Liners reconsidering their Operational Excellence to raise their Hero Intensity, it is going to require giving up some Hero Intensity in order to build your Operational Excellence.

▼ ▼ ▼

OK, that's it for the summary! You can take the Hero Factor Assessment again now if you want, or read on to learn more about your values and valuing others. And if you take the assessment and feel happy with where you land? That is OK! Not everyone can or wants to be a Hero. The only categories that are not OK are Wannabe (because you will fail if you stay there) and Zero (because, *ew*).

Remember always: Your Hero Factor is a choice, and one you must make authentically and genuinely. But it is not a choice that maintains itself. If you are happy with being a Good Co., you will still need to work to maintain your Operational Excellence and Hero Intensity to stay there. All I want is for leaders and companies to be the best version of themselves—the best they feel they can be—and keep being that way.

Actually, I lied. What I really want is for you to aspire to be more—to take a hard look at yourself and the work your company is doing and see if you can raise your Hero Factor and be the biggest hero you can possibly be.

To choose to hold yourself accountable on both levels, in balance, all the time! To see the hero in you and others and make more of them for our future. To transform what you are doing and win!

Finally, if your head is spinning a little right now, don't worry. Mine was too as I started to put this book together. I encourage you to go back and review this section regularly, especially each time you take the Hero Factor Assessment—and don't forget to have your people take it too and discuss the results with them. The Hero Factor is not meant to be definitive. It's designed to be provocative and promote discussion and force you to focus on what you really stand for and whether your people agree with you. It's OK to pick apart everything I say, tell me why I'm wrong, or call me stupid. You won't be the first or the last. But if you go into the rest of this book with that mindset, you aren't heading into the discussion trying to be a Hero. You're trying to be my Villain!

UNDERSTANDING YOUR HERO FACTOR

Take the time to answer these questions before you read on. They are the key questions I asked leaders as I put this book together, and I will ask them again in some form in the chapters to come:

▼ What does the call to hero leadership mean to you? Are you ready to pick a side?

▼ What does hero leadership/being a hero company mean to you? How do you live that? How do your people live that?

▼ Can you name what you value above all else in your work? What are your non-negotiables? What have you evolved and changed your stance on?

▼ What is the most unheroic thing you have seen a good company/leader do, and how do you stop yourself/your business from doing the same thing?

▼ What must any leader/business do to sustain itself beyond the bottom line and leave a hero legacy?

PART II

HERO INTENSITY
YOUR VALUES

Do you have values that support and help communicate a clear vision of who you are, what you expect, and where you want to go? Most leaders say they do, and I believe *they* believe that is true. After all, everyone understands the importance of having a stated purpose for your company and leadership and values that back it up. But when I ask whether those values are written down so everyone inside and outside the company can see them . . . well, that's a different story. Do you? And if you do, how do you live and demonstrate them every day? You can't fully trust and respect a leader or an organization that has no clearly stated or ever-changing values. Your values, whatever they happen to be, are the foundation of the first part of your Hero Intensity (the second being how you value others), and without them you're at best a Wannabe.

CHAPTER 5

WHAT ARE YOUR VALUES?

*T*here's a new wave of social entrepreneurs and a growing recognition of brand integrity. That you have to be more than an advertising slogan. To be real. To have values . . .

That was the opening I drafted for a letter inviting leaders to join The Hero Club. And then I stopped writing. I knew what I wanted to say. I wanted to celebrate the people and businesses that create real jobs and positively influence real communities as a result of what they produce. I wanted to build a new nation of real business heroes who made money, implemented and executed on their vision, and stood up against greed. Leaders who have the Hero Factor.

But something was missing.

I thought back to the first time I met some of the club members in person. I was participating in the 2016 Rocky Mountain Economic Summit and was invited to come a day early to give a "tent talk" to a small group before we went fly-fishing for trout, which I love as much as I love to eat them—smoked, fried, baked . . . But I digress. Anyway, it was just before the presidential election, and the tent was full of economists, hedge fund managers, millionaires, billionaires, and a few politicians. John E. Silvia, the chief economist for Wells Fargo, had asked me to speak about what I would do if Trump or Clinton asked me to be chief marketing officer of the United States of America. How would I sell the country?

I started by explaining that when you look at a brand as chief marketing officer, you have to look at it from its inception and through the lens of customer satisfaction with the product. A brand is nothing more than a promise delivered, so what's the promise America delivers? First, I said it was freedom, but I said "was," because America used to be *the* land of freedom. We still are free, but so are many other countries. The people from those countries, like most Europeans who immigrated here in the 18th and 19th centuries, are not looking to come here anymore. Their own countries deliver on that promise as well as or even better for them than we can.

After that, America manufactured things for ourselves and others within our borders. No one had better technology or entrepreneurial drive to innovate. Today, American companies manufacture the majority of the products they sell and buy outside our borders, and many international companies in countries like Israel, Finland, and Japan invest as much or more in things like research and design. We still grow much of the food we consume and may be the most modernized farming and agricultural country in the world, but we are no longer the breadbasket of the world by many measures. Brazil grows more soybeans, Russia more wheat, and we no longer export the majority of the world's corn.

So I wondered if America's brand promise is not an actual thing, but our way of life. But that "American Dream" is so different for so many and seems to be more romantic than real, the stuff of TV and movies, which may be the real answer to what we sell, along with other forms of entertainment. Yet I'd hate to think that America's brand is the fiction we create and the music we listen to to escape from reality.

So what "products" remain that make America the greatest, not just great? First, there's defense—we have the mightiest army in the world, and we make a lot of weapons to support it and our allies. But there's something else that's survived, and that's free enterprise. The way America does business has evolved. What we sell has changed. But America is still a place where businesses are by and large free to operate with a minimum of government regulation. Sure, some want more regulation, others want less, but for most investors we are just right: America is the place other countries want to put their money. They want to invest here and invest in their children by sending them to college here. We're the biggest market for everything from cola to cars to condos. Millions upon millions of Americans and people throughout the world have gotten wealthy because of it. We should celebrate that as our beacon of light.

Now I ask you: Do you think I was trying to sound more like Trump or Clinton? The answer is neither. I sounded like me—a real American and a real person who was speaking from my head and heart. I wanted The Hero Club to celebrate that in others and each other regardless of party affiliation. That was the spirit of what I wanted our organization to capture, not our values. Which is when I made a stark discovery.

WHAT WERE OUR VALUES?

The Hero Club was created by Rob Ryan, who founded Ascend Communications in 1989 and grew it to more than $2 billion in revenue over the next ten years. In 1999, Lucent Technologies acquired Ascend for approximately $20 billion, a deal that stood as the largest technology merger ever until Microsoft bought LinkedIn for $26.2 billion in 2016. The deal made Ryan a billionaire several times over.

Ryan is the very definition of the best of entrepreneurial America, and he wanted to pay it forward to make more entrepreneurs millionaires and billionaires. He did this in an extraordinary way for his employees at the time of the sale (see Chapter 16 on giving back) and another for everyone else: He ran a technology boot camp and wrote a book, *Entrepreneur America: Lessons From Inside Rob Ryan's High-Tech Start-Up Boot Camp* (Harperbusiness, 2001).

Hero Partners was something different. It was for businesspeople with the wealth and stature of Ryan, who came together to collaborate and help others maintain win-win relationships and grow, even in the shadow of the Great Recession.

Hero Partners was not for startups, however. The club wouldn't let people in unless they believed their company could generate a billion dollars in revenue. That requirement limited the club's reach and excluded many potential heroes. The vast majority of companies in America, including mine, are small businesses; no matter how well-run they are, they will never earn close to $1 billion. So in the years before I took over The Hero Club, the organization lowered its barrier to entry: As long as a company had the potential for millions of dollars in sustained and sustainable revenue and demonstrated operational excellence, they could be invited to join and benefit from working with leaders who had a size and scope of expertise they lacked.

Those were the people I was writing to at the start of this chapter, inviting them to become members of the club. But was money the qualification The Hero Club should value most? As I said in Part I, revenue used to be the sole measurement of a company's excellence. But operational excellence alone does not make you a hero today. Being a hero is about much more than the bottom line. It's about encouraging entrepreneurship in America and helping companies, their leadership, and their people be the best at what they do—and how they do it. America was built on entrepreneurship. That's the foundation of our free enterprise system, and we need to keep that spirit alive and make it the focal point of what it means to be American. The more entrepreneurship, the more American we are. (In a nod to our European Hero Club members, I will note the word *entrepreneur* was coined in France and comes from the French word *entreprendre* or *undertake*.)

I wanted that and more for our members to hang their proverbial hats on. I wanted a commitment to build companies they are proud to be a part of, beyond the bottom line. I wanted them to be proud of how they treat others, and to be proud about what and how they give back to their communities. That's when I first thought about the Hero Intensity scale in determining your Hero Factor. And that's why I stopped writing that morning: I still didn't understand what that meant in tangible terms for our potential members: What was the specific commitment I was asking them to make? What made The Hero Club stand apart? What were we asking hero leaders to *do* to develop their Hero Factors so the next generations could build more hero businesses?

What were The Hero Club's values? And I realized we didn't have any. At least not written down. So I wrote some down, and they became the first iteration of a pledge every Hero Club member makes to hero entrepreneurship, even if they lead or work for the biggest companies in the world. Remember, entrepreneurialism is a spirit—a lifestyle, if you will, one that you can pursue even when you work for the largest companies. It's about innovating and thinking outside the boardroom box—even if that's where you sit every day. Making money matters, but hero leaders and companies do it while consistently and constantly seeking out new and bigger opportunities and possibilities and being guided by a servant mentality—or, as I like to call it, stewardship.

Here is the current iteration of those Hero Club values as this book goes to press, broken down into what we pledge and the actions we take to live those values:

The Pledge of a Hero Business
▼ Communicates a clear vision of where we want to go
▼ Can implement ideas and drive change
▼ Is guided by a servant mentality to people, causes, and organizations
▼ Commits on values to all stakeholders
▼ Embraces sharing credit with teammates

▼ Owns a driving belief in sharing success and wealth

▼ Is relentless: When knocked down, we get back up!

▼ Is willing to do any job required to succeed

▼ Focuses on growth, not just lifestyle business for the CEO/ founder

The Actions of a Hero Business

▼ Exemplifies results that are outside the industry norm

▼ Has a bottom-up organization: Engages all business units in building and making the organization more efficient

▼ Is rooted in success based on values and value to its community, stakeholders, and common good

▼ Focuses on growth and maximum impact for the business and its employees

▼ Recognizes strengths and weaknesses and strives for continual improvement

▼ Performs work or builds products that inspire or disrupt the norm

▼ Exhibits transparency with a clear vision and values and is practiced throughout the organization

▼ Is valued as a brand, reflective of the promises delivered

I called these Hero Club values a pledge because one of the greatest things we do in this country is pledge allegiance to the flag. Everyone knows that pledge, and it grounds our young people every day in what it means to be part of this republic. I wanted The Hero Club pledge to ground our members in what we were doing beyond the bottom line—to be a clear commitment to acting on something we believe in. It cuts through the noise and commits our members to a life balance of hard work while giving back to their communities. It says, "This is what we value."

The pledge defines our *duty* to hero leadership and serving everyone, up and down and across your company, not just the bottom line (and certainly not Wall Street and shareholders above all else). It holds us accountable to something sustainable and consistent, yet adaptive and evolving—on both the hero side and the operational side.

> *What do you pledge yourself to? How does it balance*
> *Operational Excellence and Hero Intensity?*

Now, before we go any further, know this book is not a sales pitch for The Hero Club. (But if you want to apply, that's great—we consider all applications equally.) I am also not advocating for you to adopt our values as your own. If you like them, great. If you don't, that's OK, too. While I believe some of these values are essential to all businesses that have the Hero Factor (and will cover those in the following chapters), you can be a hero without them. You can even reject them—as long as you replace them with values that are important to *you* as a company and a leader.

And if you think you have heard some or all of the pledge before? You probably have! In fact, many Hero Club members make this pledge knowing they already do many of the things on the list. But they still take the pledge to remind themselves that they must KEEP doing them. I would say most leaders know they should do these things. *Most leaders even say they do these things.* But sometimes we fail to do them in the moments that really count. We lose sight of what we value. From time to time, we are surprised when a company does something that goes against what they *said* they valued. But when we look back, we realize those values were never there in the first place.

WHAT ARE YOUR VALUES?

The crucial point is not what my or your values are or what anyone else thinks of them, but **that they exist**, that they are clearly stated, and that we commit ourselves to them. This is why I never ask to see the values or mission statements of companies—only whether they have them written down and clearly defined. This holds for everyone, personally and professionally, and for any business, from sole proprietors to Fortune 500 companies. You'd be surprised how many people and companies don't do this. Or maybe you wouldn't, because most people don't. But your people, customers, partners, and community want to see that basic commitment in the people and companies they do business with.

You can't operationalize values in the workplace and marketplace if no one can see what they are—starting with you.

BE A HERO: WRITE OUT YOUR VALUES

Do you have the things you and your organization or team value written down? The values that you and they stand for and believe personally and professionally?

▼ If you already have those values written out, congratulations! Write them out now again *without* having them in front of you. Then take a moment to review them against the previous version and make sure they line up. If they don't, you have a disconnect at the heart of your Hero Intensity as a team/organization.

▼ If you don't have your values written out, take a moment the next time you're at work and write down the values of your organization or team. The list can be any length and have statements of any size. Remember: The point isn't to worry about what they look like or to test them but just to make sure they exist.

▼ Now take a moment and write down your personal values as a leader. Think about whether they connect and align to the values of the team/organization. Are they the same? Or are there differences? If they differ, you have a disconnect at the heart of your Hero Intensity as a leader.

I hope you found that exercise fun. I did the first time I did it. But if you also found it difficult, don't be surprised. It's much harder to write out what you stand for so everyone can see it than it is to just say it. It's going to get even harder as you test those values and the courage of your convictions in the next chapters. And if you found the exercise a little basic or what you said a little cliché—well, that's kind of the point, too. The point isn't to be unique but to lay down the values that define you.

Still need help focusing? Bring it down to the most basic level. I asked a diverse group of hundreds of CEOs and leaders of Hero Club companies large and small to list three words that define the values of being a hero leader and company. Some of them linked the three words to create a statement, like "leadership without authority" or "building better people," but Figure 5.1 shows the words that were repeated several times or more (the bigger the word, the higher the repetition).

Figure 5.1 Hero Values Word Cloud

If these words resonate with you, use them to create values that represent you and your organization. If you already have a list of values, use these words to test your values and see if, like these, they strike a balance between the two parts of the Hero Factor (Operational Excellence and Hero Intensity).

Still need help? Following are some examples of values from companies whose employees rate them highly for sticking to their values.

First, look at the values included in Chevron's "The Chevron Way," which according to the company "explains who we are, what we believe, how we achieve, and where we aspire to go. It establishes a common understanding not only for us, but for all who interact with us." Chevron says the foundation for all that is built on its values, which are:

- ▼ *Diversity and inclusion.* We learn from and respect the cultures in which we operate. We have an inclusive work environment that values the uniqueness and diversity of individual talents, experiences, and ideas.
- ▼ *High performance.* We are passionate about delivering results and strive to continually improve. We hold ourselves accountable for our actions and outcomes. We apply proven processes in a fit-for-purpose manner and always look for innovative and agile solutions.
- ▼ *Integrity and trust.* We are honest with ourselves and others and honor our commitments. We trust, respect, and support each other. We earn the trust of our colleagues and partners by operating with the highest ethical standards in all we do.
- ▼ *Partnership.* We build trusting and mutually beneficial relationships by collaborating with our communities, governments, customers, suppliers, and other business partners. We are most successful when our partners succeed with us.
- ▼ *Protect people and the environment.* We place the highest priority on the health and safety of our work force and protection of our assets, communities, and the environment. We deliver world-class performance with a focus on preventing high-consequence incidents.

Do you agree with these values? You couldn't possibly because Chevron is Big Oil? Again, that's not the point right now. The point is that they *exist*. Everyone can see what Chevron stands for on the operations side and the hero side. As an employee, partner, or customer, you are free to judge Chevron against these values. If you're expecting something outside or contrary to these values, whether you are filling your car at the pump or own the station at which that pump is located, that's not Chevron's problem.

Or consider the core values that Zappos employees live by to do what CEO Tony Hsieh wants them to do: "Deliver happiness." They pledge to:

▼ Deliver WOW through service
▼ Embrace and drive change
▼ Create fun and a little weirdness
▼ Be adventurous, creative, and open-minded
▼ Pursue growth and learning
▼ Build open and honest relationships with communication
▼ Build a positive team and family spirit
▼ Do more with less
▼ Be passionate and determined
▼ Be humble

What do you think? Did you say, "They're fine, but I don't want to work for a shoe company"? Do you think all the people who line up to work for Zappos do so because they want to sell shoes? Seriously, how many people want to sell shoes? OK, to each his or her own, but I assure you that if you care about shoes but don't live these values, you won't last long at Zappos. They make this clear, as does Chevron. That's what I want you to do as well before you continue on in this book.

But just as I didn't choose The Hero Club pledge as an ad for The Hero Club, I didn't choose Chevron and Zappos as examples because I have a stake in them, love fossil fuels and shoes, or want you to agree with the values they state as a businessperson or customer. I chose them because they are brands that most people are familiar with and can judge what they know against those clearly stated values, and because their values reflect a good balance between Operational Excellence and Hero Intensity.

Here's a final example, this time from a company you might not know: Catherine Monson, CEO of Fastsigns International Inc., the franchisor of 690 Fastsigns locations which provide custom sign and graphics products, told me how her company aligns its values with one of its premier products. There's a long, well-traveled hallway in the center of the Fastsigns office they call "Inspiration Hall." Those walls are filled with more than 125 inspirational quotes inspirational quotes that talk about or refer to the company's values and characteristics like perseverance, goal-directed behavior, and positive mental attitude. As Catherine told me: "What has happened is our franchisees are putting those kinds of quotes in their production areas to feed the minds of their employees and motivating their teams. We're a sign company, so we created signs featuring our core values: Be open and positive, act with passion, do the right thing, do what you say, and make it great. And then there's descriptions under each of those 'street signs' about what we're talking about: integrity, accountability, commitment, continuous improvement, being empathetic, being an active listener. As a result, everyone on our team knows what those values are. It's part of the culture of the company."

Simply put, values are what you make them. Everything else you do to determine your Hero Intensity comes from them: What you think is right. How your people act. How you make your people feel welcome. In my company, you can be whoever you want, and I will support you as an individual. I will include you in any way I can. But you must realize that you serve these values. You must support them to keep our culture strong, because commitment to our values—just like commitment to The Hero Club pledge—is what creates a hero company.

> *The core of a great culture must be great values—*
> *written and lived.*

Returning to the word cloud in Figure 5.1 on page 49: I make no judgment of the words you choose and the values you create from them (or any other words you decide to use)—only whether they exist or not. You must declare them—shout them from the mountaintop! (Just not when I'm hunting or fishing, please.) Remember: A brand is nothing more than a promise delivered. The values that define your brand ground you in that promise—to the kind of company and leader you want to be and commit to becoming in an authentic way. If you change them inauthentically or in a desperate attempt to survive, you might keep your head above water for a while, but you'll eventually drown. Because if your values are inauthentic, so is everything you do and create. Values are what attract the best people to us, even if we disagree on what they value or even annoy us sometimes. I can't tell you how many times I have hopelessly longed for Chick-fil-A on a Sunday. But every store is closed on Sundays as part of the company's values, which focus on providing better work-life balance for its employees. I'm not happy about it most of the time, but I respect their choice—and so do the people who work for them.

Which brings me to my next point: While values ground you in the "promise" part of my brand definition, how you live your values grounds you in the "delivered" part. Your people need to live your values genuinely, top to bottom, to be believed and trusted. This may not be the case anymore (if it ever was) for people in politics, especially in Washington, DC. But in business, it matters more than ever.

CHAPTER 6

HOW ARE YOUR VALUES LIVED?

Topgolf is a global sports entertainment brand built on four key pillars: play, food, music, and community. Erik Anderson, executive chairman of Topgolf Entertainment Group, told me the company's values are built on its stated purpose to connect people in meaningful ways—a purpose that extends from its office locations to the associates taking care of guests at the venues. "That's how we come together and how we make decisions large and small," says Anderson. "Our brand purpose is our north star every day." The goal of that connection, according to Anderson? "To create moments that matter for everyone. I try and model that, looking for opportunities to highlight that by recognizing my people and seeing how we treat each other."

That sounds great. But I have heard something similar from countless leaders, and when I press them on how they do that, I quickly find that it's far easier to say what your purpose and values are than to show how you live them. A surefire way to separate the doers from the pretenders is to ask them for an example. Not necessarily the *best* example, just *an* example of how their people live what they say. The ones who can't think of one or hem and haw that "there are too many to choose just one" are often making excuses for not knowing what they should know—whether and how their people live their values.

> *It's easier to say what you value in words than to operationalize those values, sustain them, and drive them through your organization.*

Thus I was a little wary when Anderson said there are tens of thousands of examples he could choose from. But his company does serve more than 13 million guests a year, so it was possible he wasn't exaggerating. I'm glad I listened. "My favorite example," he told me, "was about an 11-year-old girl. She was having a birthday party, and she didn't like the guacamole. Now the thing you might expect to happen is we offer to take it off the check or offer to substitute something for her. But our associates saw this, told our executive chef at the location, and that chef came up from the kitchen, brought avocados, limes, jalapenos, onions, tomatoes, and a bowl, and said, 'I hear you don't like the guacamole. Why don't we make some together?' And they made this great guacamole. You can't script that."

Exactly. For a moment like that to happen, the people working for Topgolf had to go beyond what was expected—they had to live that. "That's where the power of the word *create* comes in," adds Anderson. "It wasn't about making the situation OK. It was finding the creative spirit and insight and being willing to take the time to actually do it. We can observe and participate, but creation is a critical part of the human condition. You create experiences. It ended up being an exceptional moment for that young girl."

VALUES ARE MORE THAN WORDS

Anderson's story is no more about guacamole than Zappos values from Chapter 5 are about selling shoes. Values go beyond the product to the people who deliver on the promise you make. Do you have a guacamole moment? A moment when you saw your people live your values—or when *you* lived them as more than words?

Remember what I said before: One act—big or small—does not define a hero. It takes countless little acts like these—acts an organization and its leaders value and hold themselves accountable for creating—to raise your Hero Intensity. An operationally excellent company that has no interest in being more than a Bottom Liner does not worry about creating that experience for others. Creating great experiences, let alone great cultures that are inclusive and organizations that truly give back in exceptional ways? That requires your people to understand, pay attention to, and/or do the following things, which are hard to break out when it comes to the bottom line and measure using traditional metrics and key performance indicators:

▼ A belief that what they are doing serves the purpose of the company and others
▼ How they treat customers and make them feel
▼ Seeing each deal as a relationship, not a transaction
▼ The mood and effectiveness of meetings
▼ How they respond to changes—lining up with enthusiasm or resisting
▼ Smiles—the expressions on people's faces when you look around the office
▼ Doing more than they are told—not just checking the box for a paycheck

We'll cover all these things in Part III of the book (how you value others), but for now, a hero company and leader know those things are invaluable in ways that go beyond traditional metrics but can be felt in the culture of the business and the loyalty of your people. And it all starts with your values.

Wait, you thought loyalty was defined by a big paycheck? Maybe for some—and Struggling Do-Gooders who overvalue Hero Intensity and can't make payday or product delivery deadlines will find their loyalty equally tested. For most, however, how people feel about your company and brand defines their loyalty. They want to feel valued by your organization and believe its values are genuine. Treat people like a commodity, and they'll act like one. Sure, they'll take your money, but without that Hero Intensity, those people (especially the top talent) will be gone the first opportunity they get. Maybe sooner!

Again, it's OK to choose to be a Bottom Liner—making a cursory nod to Hero Intensity and worshiping Operational Excellence. What's not acceptable is to claim hero values for PR or marketing purposes, and then when a scandal breaks, apologizing and hoping everyone forgets when the news dies down. For example, as I write this book, McDonald's has recently joined the long list of companies being accused of having a culture rife with sexual harassment. McDonald's immediately put out the statement you would expect: that there is no place for sexual harassment at the company. But apparently there is, because if that is something the company values, its people are not living it. They might be saying it, but they don't live it. It's not authentic.

> *Heroes don't just define what they believe in.*
> *They live it, genuinely and daily.*

To find that authenticity, do something similar to what Meg Manke, senior partner at management consulting company Rose Group International, did when she was a human resources and training manager for a mining company: "I think the thing that really tells you whether or not you're on the right track is what people say about you and your business at the bar," she says. "Because when people are a few beers in—or even if they're not—they're just comfortable enough to talk about things the way they want to talk about them. That's where you hear the most important things. Being in HR, I kind of based the success of the year in terms of employee engagement on the conversations that we would have. So if you had people who were saying, 'You know, I just don't really feel good about this, or we worked too many hours, or the equipment doesn't run right, or I don't like these policy changes,' I would kind of know that we had to straighten some of that stuff up. I will say, more often than not, of

---

BE A HERO: KNOW, LIVE, AND TEST YOUR VALUES

The baseline for seeing if your perceptions of your values and how they are being lived as they apply to the Hero Factor is to have your people take the Hero Assessment online via The Hero Factor book, The Hero Club, or The Hayzlett Group. Then take the following steps to reveal or resolve any disconnects:

▼ Even if they are available in writing online or around the office, ask your people to write out the values your organization/team lives by and your values as a leader. Do they align with what you wrote in Chapter 5?

▼ Now go to some of your customers and people you connect to in the community and ask them to write out what they think your values are. Do they align?

▼ Finally, ask your people to give *specific* examples or stories of how they, you, and the team/organization live those values.

Make an appointment—a real appointment—to do this exercise as soon as possible. Don't wait a year. That could be too late.

---

course it was good. When you have an inspired employee, 10, 12, 15 percent extra effort means a huge thing to the bottom line. But it's not something that can be measured the same way traditional performance indicators are."

Later we'll discuss the more complicated issue of what happens when the values of the company—not black-and-white operational issues like safety or illegal activities—and the people who work for it are misaligned. In those cases, it comes down to a question of people and organizations living their genuine values and deciding whether they can align those values or whether the organization expects complete conformity on the part of its people. There are different consequences for each, but sometimes it's just a question of understanding that need for balance.

If "balance" seems too close to the elusive notion of work/life balance, think of it as Rob Beyer, president and CEO of EarthBend, does: blending, which is what he did when he acquired some companies and integrated them, both in terms of Operational Excellence (demanding performance) and Hero Intensity (understanding how people work today): "You hear 'balance' all the time, but I don't believe in balance. I believe in blending," he says. "I'm OK with a parking lot being empty at 3 P.M., and then it's full at 7 P.M. Or people are golfing during the week and then working on weekends. That's a hero company that trusts you to get your job done. You need to train them and trust them to deliver. If I tell you that you need to be to Duluth by 6 P.M. on Friday, I'm not going to tell you how to get to Duluth. You may take a train, you may take a bike—I don't care."

For Rob and many of the hero companies I spoke to, finding a way to hold your people accountable to both sides of the Hero Factor and empowering them to act was key. Every day in business, you and your people are confronted by the opportunity to serve the organization and others and do the right thing—or the wrong thing. *Every* day, whatever right and wrong is for you, as defined by your values. How you run a meeting, how you negotiate with a vendor, how you coach your people, how you treat an 11-year-old girl who says she hates your guacamole . . . What you or your people *choose* to do next defines how your leaders and the people who follow them live the values of the organization.

Original Hero Club member Jerry Henley, CEO of Rubicon Capital, told me that when he is looking to invest in a company, "If your people are drones, then I usually get that your company's a drone."

Jerry's line conjured up memories for me of an old *Saturday Night Live* bit that spoofed all the commercials for Broadway shows that had over-the-top enthusiastic people talking about how much they loved a show. The *SNL* commercial was for a hypnotist, The Amazing Alexander, and all the people kept repeating the same words, clearly under hypnosis: "I loved it. It was much better than *Cats*. I'm going to see it again and again."

That's not how you want your values lived. That's one of the first symptoms of being stuck in your story.

CHAPTER 7

GETTING STUCK IN YOUR STORY

At one meeting, the team responsible for the email newsletter that goes to our paid membership—our primary way of communicating with those members—reported a 60 percent open rate in the first 48 hours. They actually seemed satisfied with that result—pleased, even. I, shall we say, was neither. *Let me show you how we are going to go out of business . . .*

Sixty percent? That's a D-minus! A 60 percent open rate would be astounding if this was just a piece of direct marketing designed to promote something. But a 60 percent open rate by people who *paid* to get the information from us was terrible, especially for what we felt was an important, good product. That meant 40 percent of our members weren't getting everything they paid for. *What's that? You say our members are really busy?* By that logic, 40 percent of our members don't value what we offer enough to read it—that we're a distraction to indulge when they have nothing else to do. *Oh, you think it might have gone into some members' spam folders?* That doesn't make me think they value it, either. *Some people might be away?* Maybe—but 40 percent of them?

Sure, all those reasons were plausible, but to me, all they did was add up to excuses for a near failure—reasons why not, rather than ways forward. I left the meeting disappointed. As I headed back to my desk, I thought about what actions we could take, when a Zach Galifianakis line from the movie *Due Date* popped into my head: "You better check yourself before you wreck yourself." Yes, hip hop connoisseurs, I later found out he was paraphrasing a line from an Ice Cube song. But the meaning in both instances is the same: Stop, take a step back, and think about what you're doing before things get much worse. In other words, don't get so stuck in the story of your values, who you are, and what you're doing that you lose perspective on what you are *actually* doing.

This goes beyond "look before you leap" when it comes to your Hero Factor. It's not about looking or leaping but "selling your story": telling people how great you are at looking and leaping—without making sure you're really doing either! In the case of the newsletter, I asked myself: What really bothered me most about what had happened? That we had a crappy open rate or that my team was satisfied with that open rate? Of course it was the latter. The former is a problem with results (Operational Excellence); the latter is a problem with mindset (Hero Intensity).

Simply put, my team was stuck in a story of our values, not living them. In this specific case, they weren't living one of our core values— to "be relentless" in delivering results—and I was guilty of believing they were.

The newsletter incident was another "mirror moment" for me as a leader and is a huge Hero Factor problem lurking in the background of the best companies. Sure, every one of my people knew our values included being relentless, but their satisfaction with those mediocre results revealed to me that we were not living that value. Moreover, I was not doing as good a job as I should have been to make sure we were living that value: *How many other values were we only supposedly living? How much had it cost us in Operational Excellence and Hero Intensity?* **When did it become just a story we sell to others about our values, not a story we live?**

What's the difference?

- ▼ *Living the story* of your values that says "this is who we are" is a positive.
- ▼ *Selling this story* to your people, customers, community, and beyond as part of your brand promise and identity is also a positive.
- ▼ *Failing to live the story of your values but still selling it as your story—* unable to question or see that—is a sure sign you are stuck in it.

> *Do you review your values regularly,*
> *testing that they are being lived?*

The Operational Excellence side of getting stuck in your story has been well-covered by me and others. It's the failure to innovate and adapt, especially while generating massive revenue for existing products, which leads to the decimation or death of the company when the marketplace evolves or disappears. It is the story of Kodak and film, BlackBerry and mobile communications, Blockbuster and video, Sears and retail, Yahoo! and the web.

But the Hero Intensity side of getting stuck in your story can be equally if not more devastating. It's harder to spot because we initially treat the problem as a purely operational issue, rather than one having to do with values and people. It's like spotting a mouse in your house: You may see only one, but there are probably dozens more you don't see. Treat a "stuck in your story" problem that way, and you'll fix only the problem you see, not the bigger problem having to do with your mindset. You might get results in the short run, but the larger problem does not go away and could eventually cost you much more.

I could have dismissed the newsletter issue as an isolated incident. But I knew better. I needed to make sure this wasn't happening in other teams and with other values throughout the company. If everyone is stuck in a story about your values instead of actually living them, and you don't see it until it's too late, then even the best company can find itself defending its values in the court of public opinion.

That's exactly what was happening to one of America's most recognizable and progressive brands as I wrote this book.

GETTING STUCK IN THE STORY YOU SELL

On May 29, 2018, Starbucks closed more than 8,000 company-owned stores for several hours for training on unconscious or anti-racial bias. The goal, the company said on Twitter, was to learn "how to make Starbucks a place where all people feel welcome . . . [and] renew our promise to make Starbucks an inclusive gathering place for all." As I said in Part I, a brand is nothing more than a promise delivered. Renewing a promise—like renewing wedding vows—indicates that the promise previously existed. Starbucks clearly realized it had failed to deliver on its promise of inclusivity and thus failed its brand. Good for them for connecting those dots. But if Starbucks had that promise of inclusivity as a core part of its values, why did it take so long for the company to realize all customers were not feeling welcomed?

Because Starbucks got stuck in its story.

To refresh your memory (though you'd have had to be in a coma to have missed this story completely), the training was put in place following an April 12, 2018, incident in a Philadelphia Starbucks that made and stayed in the national news for weeks afterward.

Here are the facts of what happened, which no one disputes. Two black men entered a Starbucks in a predominantly white area of Philadelphia, asked to use the bathroom, were told it was for paying customers only, and instead sat at a table without immediately ordering anything. The manager, who is white, told the men to order something or leave, and when they didn't, within minutes called 911 saying she had "two gentlemen refusing to make a purchase or leave." Like a game of Telephone, the 911 operator turned "two gentlemen" into "a group of men" and their refusal to leave into "a disturbance." A one-car response became a multiple-unit response. The first two officers entered the store and confronted the men, who remained seated. They asked what they had done wrong several times, and the officers said only that they needed to leave or they would be arrested for trespassing.

Minutes passed, and more officers arrived, as did a third man, who questioned what was going on. The man, who was white, as were all the officers, said that the two men were waiting to meet with him. They hadn't bought anything because he had wanted to buy them coffee when he arrived. He motioned to the two black men and said they could just go somewhere else. But it was too late; the police cleared the tables and chairs from around the two men and arrested them, leading them away in handcuffs without incident, save their friend screaming, "Does anybody else think this is ridiculous?" Apparently, Starbucks did: The company refused to press charges, and after being photographed and fingerprinted, the men were released eight hours later.

All the above information is taken from multiple reports from customers and employees who were there (including the manager), the actual 911 call, the two black men, police statements, and of course cell phone videos. Those videos went viral fast, and the social media response was swift and furious, with calls for everything from boycotting Starbucks to demanding justice for the two men. The company immediately apologized to the two men, CEO Kevin Johnson met with them, and five days after the incident it announced plans for the 175,000 employees at those 8,000-plus stores to spend an afternoon participating in large and small group anti-bias training guided by Starbucks chairman Howard Schultz and activist-musician Common and developed with the help of the NAACP, the Anti-Defamation League, former attorney general Eric Holder, and others. In May 2018, Starbucks settled with the men for an undisclosed amount and, according to a company statement, "continued listening and dialogue between the parties and specific action and opportunity."

The time from incident to company-wide training was just under eight weeks, and during that time Starbucks became front-page fodder, not to mention a lightning rod for professional pundits and anyone with a Facebook page or Twitter handle. No one—not the manager, the men, the police, or Starbucks—was safe from attack. People from all sides read what they wanted to see in every detail.

But forget about the police, the men, the manager, everything. I don't care about any of that for this book. Starbucks' problems didn't start that day. The company had to be stuck in its story long before then.

Say what you will about Starbucks' coffee—how it tastes, how much it costs, the calories in a venti Frappuccino with whipped cream—the story of the company behind the coffee has been good to great in terms of Operational Excellence, with increased revenues every year since 2009. Its Hero Intensity story has arguably been even stronger. For example, the company long ago gave employees who work an average of 20 hours a week access to the same health insurance as salaried employees. It offers everything from benefits for domestic partners to adoption assistance. It even has a long history of being a pioneer in launching stores in urban minority areas. In 1998, former basketball player Magic Johnson persuaded then-CEO Howard Schultz to sell him franchises in inner-city neighborhoods across the country. In 2010, the company bought them back at a premium, and to this day, like many of Starbucks' urban properties, almost all of those stores remain profitable.

But what really made Starbucks a hero to its customers was not getting people, regardless of race, to pay $4 for a cup of coffee but *not paying for it*. Part of Starbucks' mission has been to be a "Third Place," which Starbucks told CNET in 2009 meant creating "a welcoming environment for all our customers. We do not have any time limits for being in our stores and continue to focus on making the Third Place experience for every Starbucks customer." Howard Schultz reaffirmed this Third Place ideal in a 2013 letter to customers about Starbucks being a place between home and work where people can gather to enjoy "coffee and community" with no apparent restriction on tables and bathrooms, whether you are a paying or nonpaying customer.

I'm sure Starbucks has its reasons. Unlike independent coffee shops, its stores can afford to do that as part of its marketing. So their purpose for existence isn't totally altruistic—they're a full-on capitalistic company, and I respect that. But before I continue, let me say I don't get the idea of treating paying and nonpaying customers equally. I believe that if you don't buy something in a place, you ought not be there. If I have to use the restroom and pop into a Starbucks, I will come out after washing my hands and buy something small as a thank-you, like a pack of gum, which I will never, ever chew. Because that's what my mom taught me: If you use a place of business, you should buy something.

Which is what those two men in Philadelphia were going to do that day once their third companion got there, but while they didn't, according to Starbucks' values, they should still have been totally welcome. Now I've heard that people have started calling any incidents of white people calling the police on black people for simply living their lives being "Starbucked."

How did a company that by many measures had been living its values get to this point? My belief is Starbucks has lived in that Third Place ideal for a long time, but in a time when America is more polarized and tribal than ever, it never tested if its people were living that ideal with *all* its customers. Starbucks assumed all was well. Like my team with the newsletter, it convinced itself that everything was OK. It said to itself, "Hey, we're in our Starbucks story. This is who we are. This is what we do." And then, boom! The company finds out its people stopped living the story it has been selling every day. That's

> *Every company sells a story about its values.*
> *Are you still living yours every day?*

when you have to stop, reset, and not only say who you are, but also ensure it is being lived top to bottom.

Starbucks' response indicated it understood the problem immediately. When something like this happens, how a company reacts is a true test of its authentic Hero Intensity. Starbucks passed that test, in my opinion: It said, without defensiveness or blaming anyone else, "We're not like that—that's not us! How could this happen?" before asking, "Holy ****! What's this going to do to the company?"

CHECK YOURSELF BEFORE YOU WRECK YOURSELF

Anyone who thinks Starbucks overreacted to one bad apple employee or sees the training as just a PR stunt or mea culpa writ large is missing my point. Any small incident can become an international scandal in the age of social media, and bad apples are like that mouse in your house: There is never just one. So before you go pointing fingers, I ask you:

▼ Can any among us say we have done all we can to shake ourselves out of the stories we write for ourselves? That means doing more than addressing the problem (apologize for our bad behavior or fire the offending employee); we have to address the mindset that created a culture that allowed the problem to happen.

▼ Can any among us say we constantly review our values to make sure that we are actually living them?

▼ Can any among us say we have not used a story to explain why we can't do something or why we got the results we did?

If you answered yes to all these questions, then surely you got or will get and give yourself tens on the Hero Intensity scale. That's

> *An apology is not enough to change your story.*
> *One act is not enough either. You must keep writing.*

great! I salute you. Now what will you do to maintain that score? I'm sure Starbucks thought it was close to tens, too. Then a single 911 call from a manager led not only to a public relations nightmare but also accusations that struck at the heart of the story of its values. Yes, Starbucks' response was a bit of a show and had its fair share of criticism that it was just another corporate act of compliance. Of course, one day of training will not undo the bias we are all guilty of unless it is followed up and sustained. But at least Starbucks is taking immediate steps to start writing the story of its values again.

The Starbucks incident shows that you can always be surprised—that you're often only as good as your weakest link. On some level, Starbucks is asking, as a company that has hero values in other areas, how many of these bad apples—or potential ones—exist? There may be degrees of problems and complicity, but how many of these people do they *not* know about because they got stuck in their story?

Simply put, Starbucks is holding itself accountable. It made a choice to do more. In the end, it must know it will never have 100 percent customer satisfaction—no one will—and there's always going to be some bad apples, but how Starbucks handled it is obviously a sign of who it is as a company. It strengthened its Hero Intensity and puts its values to the test.

Remember: It's often not a question of Starbucks or any other company lacking values. Many companies facing scandals had value statements that ran contrary to the cultures that created those problems. You now have those value statements too, and it's easy to get stuck in them if you don't constantly test them—to choose to turn the spotlight of accountability on yourself.

Catherine Jackson, a former senior vice president at the global financial company Macquarie Group before she launched the mobile tech travel startup My Fave Places, understands exactly what I mean, especially when it comes to another company that is turning the spotlight of accountability on itself: "Wells Fargo was clearly just terrible with millions of fake accounts, but the sales staff were under such pressure to do that," she says. "What about yours? How are your staff measured on their success? What are the pressures that they're under? How is management held accountable? Where are the conversations around this? Wells Fargo can be dismissed as a big bank, but you can actually look at it and reflect on it in your own company and say, 'Well, how could we get into a situation like that, where staff are doing something they know is wrong, like either manipulating or feeling they have to manipulate figures in order to get incentives and bonuses?'"

Many companies not only don't do what Catherine says but also abdicate all responsibility. Accountability does not come from saying,

---

BE A HERO: CHECK YOURSELF IN THE MIRROR

This is your wakeup call to take a step back and really check you're not stuck in your hero story before you take a fall. The easiest way to do that is to gather your team and ask them and yourself two questions. The first one is much easier to answer than the second:

1. What's the most unheroic thing you've seen a company do that ran contrary to your values, and how do we stop our business or ourselves from doing the same thing?

2. What's the most unheroic thing you've seen *our* company do that ran contrary to our values, and how did we stop it from happening again—or how can we stop it now if it is still happening?

It may be tough to get an honest or even any answer from your people if they do not feel free to speak up (see Chapters 9 and 10), so take note of that if you are met with silence. If they say, "Nothing!" and smile politely, that doesn't mean you're perfect. It means you have a bigger Hero Intensity problem than you thought because your people won't tell you what they know.

"Who am I to judge?" as an excuse for your company or someone else doing something that truly goes against your values. So before you go wagging a finger at someone else, maybe have your own mirror moment.

Need help getting started? How about asking yourself how you deal with mistakes: When was the last time you admitted making a mistake, and how did you handle it? That was a common question from our Hero Club leaders. Here are a couple of common mistakes our members offered that they often see in others:

- ▼ Brigham Dickinson, president and founder Power Selling Pros and Power Certification, a customer-experience training program: "Give credit and take blame: You rarely accomplish anything by yourself. When you succeed, give credit to your team. When there is a pitfall, take upon yourself not just the blame but the resolve to make sure it doesn't happen again."
- ▼ Tom Landry, president of Allegiance Staffing: "When you sponsor a cause, you often get an opportunity to speak at an event. What I consistently see people do is get up there and give a five-minute commercial about their company. That to me is the rudest, stupidest thing I've ever seen. Instead of saying why you're involved in the charity and promoting the charity or promoting the function and giving some gratitude for actually being there and being thankful for the ability to help and try to support it, you turn it all about you."

If you need help turning that spotlight on yourself, consider what Bill Baker, a technology-turned-media entrepreneur whose current projects include Celebrity Food Network, told me about getting stuck in his own story: He was an unheroic CEO 20 years ago, and it still haunts him: "I started a little company and that company became a multinational. I went from being Bootstrap Bill to Broadband Bill, a number-one competitor of Cisco, self-funded, multinational, 120-something employees. Had an opportunity to sell the startup I co-founded to a publicly traded company called Cascade

Communications for around $250 million. And I said no. Ninety percent of my employees would have been millionaires. I said no because Broadband Bill wanted to be a Billionaire Bill. That didn't happen. Eventually we still sold, but unfortunately, I disappointed a lot of people. And I made myself a promise that I was never, ever, ever going to do that ever again and now offer a better-than-average employee participation program. But still, when I think about it, it brings tears in my eyes because I could have changed a hundred lives. Forever. I was that hero who went to zero."

OK, most of us will never face that brutal a wakeup call to take a step back and really check you're not stuck in your hero story before you take a fall. Here are three things you can do right now to do more than react when something bad happens, check on how your values are being lived, and avoid that Hero Factor fall:

1. Look for opportunities, not excuses.
2. Visit with your people—walk around!
3. Get to know who your people are and what they can do.

Look for Opportunities, Not Excuses

From the seeming inability to hire more diverse faculty to the exposure of abuse by people associated with Penn State (of young football players) and Michigan State (of young gymnasts), universities are among the most resistant organizations to deal with problems, admit mistakes, and adapt. They make every excuse in the wake of these scandals, from bureaucracy to the lack of qualified candidates to playing the blame game, or they just fail to admit they ignored or refused to take seriously the nature of the complaints and evidence. So I was really taken aback (in a good way) when I read an article in *The Washington Post* by Marybeth Gasman, a professor of higher education in the Graduate School of Education at the University of Pennsylvania, who answered the question, "Why aren't college faculties more racially diverse?" with an unbelievably honest answer: "The reason we don't have more faculty of color among college faculty is that we don't want them. We simply don't want them."

In other words, they want people like themselves (white, liberal, mostly male) and find every reason they can to dismiss the others. They look for every reason "why not" to keep writing the story they have for centuries. This is the biggest impediment to inclusive leadership, which we will cover in Chapter 13. For now, remember if you keep fishing in the same spot, you will likely catch what you always have, which may be a lot. But others may take the time to fish elsewhere or partner with people and organizations that know where to catch bigger, better, or different fish and give them expertise and increased Operational Excellence you don't have.

What do I mean by that? Consider the most recognizable name in health care: the Mayo Clinic. On the May 24, 2018, edition of the syndicated radio show *Marketplace*, Dr. John Noseworthy, president and CEO of the Mayo Clinic, talked about "entrepreneurial plans" for a hospital that opened in 1889, so it doesn't get stuck in its story for its next century in business. He encourages physicians and scientists to be entrepreneurs and to collaborate as teams to solve problems without compromising the bond between physician and patient. He is open to artificial intelligence. And he doesn't see a threat in Amazon, JPMorgan Chase, and Berkshire Hathaway potentially getting into the health-care field. He sees it as an opportunity: "We don't have a high-quality, sustainable, affordable health-care system in America," he said on the show. "And folks are looking at that and saying, 'What could I bring to that?' Of course, Amazon, JPMorgan Chase, and Berkshire Hathaway can bring capital, logistics, know-how, technology, price transparency, and they've reached out to us and we've talked with them about what the opportunities are, and I think there are great opportunities there."

Visit with Your People—Walk Around!

Whether you have walls and doors or cubicles, sit in the corner office or in the center of it all, when you work in one place, you only see what's around you. When was the last time you walked around your offices—every part of them? I'm talking the server rooms and shipping, manufacturing and accounting, sales and marketing, and IT and inventory. Not to spy on your people, but to learn, engage, understand . . . see how your story is being lived! Try it out. Have the team leader show you around and do the following:

▼ Look for things going right—and what you don't understand.
▼ Ask questions to learn.
▼ Make sure you keep doing it to maintain that connection to your story.

Catherine Monson understands the power these visits have to reinforce the values you hold and drive them through the culture of your business. She was hired to be the CEO of Fastsigns International in 2008 by the private equity firm that bought the company from the founder. She felt blessed to follow in that founder's footsteps but noted he had some different philosophies: He rarely went out in the field visiting franchisees, or what some leaders call MBWA—Management By Walking Around.

"I'm always in the field visiting franchisees," Catherine says. "I do that for lots of reasons. I do so to learn what's really happening out there, to build relationships, to use the opportunity to motivate and influence them to do something to increase their success. Because sometimes when you have the CEO title, you have more impact. One of my early mentors talked about the impact of MBWA, and so now when I'm in the corporate office, I'm wandering around, too. I'm talking to people on the team, no matter if they're direct reports—and, more important, if they're not my direct reports—and ask, 'How are things going? Do you have the tools you need? What's your biggest challenge today? How are we supporting you in solving that challenge?'

"I also do that with franchisees when I'm out in the field. When I visited Wisconsin to do a ribbon cutting for our new franchisee in Waukesha, Wisconsin, I also visited franchisees in Racine, Kenosha, and Glendale. Why? Because I want to be face-to-face and belly-to-belly out there, whether it's with team members or with franchisees. That's all part of influencing and building relationships."

Connect with the People Who Do the Work

Anyone who has seen an episode of *Undercover Boss*, in which CEOs go undercover at their own companies to do the lowest-paying jobs, understands how easy it is to get disconnected as your company grows. So make it a point to reconnect and ensure your people are not stuck in their stories. If you don't ask, you might still see the results—good and bad—but you'll never understand the mindset of the people creating those results.

As Pirooz Abir, CEO of domestic and international payment processing company LiquidInvoice LLC, said to me: "If you're leading an organization, you may not know the exact job of each person within the organization. But if you do not understand what they're producing, you can brush them off. Bottom line is you need to know the value each person is bringing to your teams. You need to understand that they put the hours in to make some software work or some application work or some customer work. As a leader, you better know what your flock is doing. You may not know the exact work [they're doing], but you better know what they're up to, how they have worked, and when they have put their heart and soul into the business to get you where you are. You better thank them."

And when you do, listen to the way they talk about others and how successful the team is, vs. what they have done by themselves, and keep that in mind as we go into Part III. But before we do, know that getting stuck in your story is not necessarily a negative—if you are aware of what you are doing. For example, refusing to work with people and companies because they are too different from you to fit with you personally (as opposed to not sharing your values) or their lack of likeability is too much to bear. But there is a "Zero Hero" quality to remaining willfully ignorant of problems with people or partners under the guise of staying true to your values, and a Zero Hero quality to not looking at your values and seeing if any need updating, refreshing, or changing.

There is, however, a *real* Hero quality to having the courage of your convictions when your values are tested.

CHAPTER 8

THE **COURAGE OF** YOUR **CONVICTIONS**

Imagine if having courage was your core value—if it defined your very existence and was *the* promise your brand delivered on. Consider the story of some of the toughest, bravest, most skilled heroes of all time: the Native American warriors known as the Dog Soldiers. The Dog Soldiers were the Cheyenne tribe's best offense and last line of defense. No tribe moved its camp or hunting ground without the Dog Soldiers leading the way and protecting the rear from attack. But these warriors were not only courageous, they were kind and good: In between battles, they fed and watched over those in need of help.

Those who have known me for a while or read my second

book, *Running the Gauntlet*, know of my reverence for the Dog Soldiers. But as I contemplated what it meant to have the courage to stand for your values while maintaining your kindness and goodness, I found myself looking at them differently—as "nevá'hanéhe" (the Cheyenne word for hero) and true embodiments of the Hero Factor in their time. They delivered Operational Excellence: Their arrows went straighter and farther than any other and anchored them in battle. When the time came to fight, they tied one end of a sacred sash around themselves and drove the other end into the ground with one of their arrows. There they remained until it was time to advance, the battle was done, or they were killed. No retreat. A courageous heart like that, coupled with the way they served all tribe members, gave them a powerful Hero Intensity: No one valued others more or cared more about what they stood for.

For all this and more, the Dog Soldiers were held in the highest

---

Fear is a reaction. Courage is a choice.

---

regard. Children looked up to them. Tribesmen respected them. Their power was indisputable, their virtue unquestionable, and their courage undeniable. That courage was non-negotiable.

Yours must be, too, in the service of your core values.

STANDING UP FOR WHAT YOU TRULY VALUE

Hero leaders and companies always have a big vision that they pursue every day, and their values inform that vision. In the service of those values, they need to:

- ▼ Live their values
- ▼ Hold themselves responsible and accountable to their values every day
- ▼ Create a culture that reflects their values
- ▼ Think bigger and better than they already do and differently

than they have before

▼ Welcome and actually listen to dissenting voices—not just the ones who affirm what you already believe

▼ Be willing to learn from others without thinking that new knowledge and nuance undermine what they believe

▼ Admit they don't know it all

▼ See opportunities for partnerships and relationships in their people and the community that allow them to grow as businesses and leaders

▼ Be willing to sacrifice and compromise

▼ Be good and kind in how they treat others

We have already covered or will cover all these points in this book. For now, know all those things require flexibility and vulnerability, not to mention dedication and time. But while things like sacrifice and compromise are essential in how we work—even when it comes to our values, as we will see in the next chapter—there must be some values we will never compromise. Our core values are the ones that anchor us, our people, and our organizations and give us the courage to keep standing and fighting. They are our Dog Soldier arrows in the ground. Our non-negotiables. No hero can operate successfully or have Hero Intensity without them.

That means you can never be in the middle when it comes to these values. I love the scene in *The Karate Kid* where Mr. Miyagi explains to Daniel that deciding to learn karate is like crossing the street: "Walk on road? Walk right side, safe. Walk left side, safe. Walk middle, sooner or later get the squish just like grape." Walk middle when it comes to the courage of your convictions, to try and appease two sides? Squish, just like grape.

So what is non-negotiable for you? And I mean never, ever, lest your Hero Intensity take a massive tumble. *Do you have the courage to stand up for those values when challenged? When others don't understand? When people complain or drag your name through the mud? When they say they won't do business with you?*

None of those things matters more than having the courage to "live like you are"—that is, authentically living the values you will not compromise. And that takes courage, especially to stand up for them when they're attacked. To be like the Dog Soldiers and face whatever foe is in front of you, triumph, and move forward to fight again and again and again . . . because that is living who you are with values and purpose. That's being a warrior.

WHAT ARE YOU NON-NEGOTIABLE ON?

I am a huge fan of Ray Dalio and his philosophy of radical transparency. The concept of "radical transparency" is not new, but Dalio has made it almost an art form. He believes everything goes on the table. *Everything*. Nothing is hidden. From giving feedback to how you treat others, nothing is held back. The point is to be free to disagree, say what you mean, and hear it back about yourself and others. This extends to recruiting future talent. If a leader and team think a potential employee can be a rock star but can't abide by the radical transparency standard, they are not hired, no matter how many dollars they bring to the table. No exceptions. This, Dalio argues, creates an environment of trust. Does that mean his business is a hero company? Perhaps. Valuing transparency does not necessarily create a culture that values others. But it certainly has not affected his company's Operational Excellence: His Bridgewater Associates is the largest hedge fund in the world, managing around $160 billion in assets.

Dalio has the courage of his convictions when it comes to valuing radical transparency. He and his people live it and drive it through the organization every day, unwaveringly. For those who don't have millions to invest with Bridgewater and experience it firsthand, you can still see examples of it every day. Take the one I mentioned previously that has caused me great culinary consternation. Chick-fil-A states on every sign, "Closed Sundays" and has since it was founded in 1967. Because of the outspoken, conservative religious views of its founder, Truett Cathy, this is often seen as related to a core value of his Christianity, but it's actually a bigger value about the need to rest. It comes from having worked in restaurants that operated 24/7. According to the company, Cathy wanted Sunday to be a day "that he and his employees could set aside . . . to rest and worship if they choose" and "be with family and friends."

Or consider the outdoor retailer REI: It may be open every day of the week during the year, but breaking with recent retail tradition, it not only closes on Thanksgiving (so its people and customers can spend time around the table with family and friends) but also on Black Friday (so they can #OptOutside and enjoy the gear they already have).

> *A value that is non-negotiable is exactly that. It must be consistently and courageously defended when tested, or it is no longer non-negotiable.*

Or what about Starbucks and its stance on guns? I accused Starbucks of getting stuck in its story in Chapter 7, but in 2013, it decided to write a different story that absolutely alienated some of its customers: Recognizing the gun debate had become dangerously polarizing in our current contentious political climate, Starbucks "respectfully" requested that its customers not bring guns into its stores. As Howard Schultz wrote on the company's website: "Pro-gun activists have used our stores as a political stage for media events misleadingly called 'Starbucks Appreciation Days' that disingenuously portray Starbucks as a champion of 'open carry.' To be clear: we do not want these events in our stores. Some anti-gun activists have also played a role in ratcheting up the rhetoric and friction, including soliciting and confronting our customers and partners. For these reasons, today we are respectfully requesting that customers no longer bring firearms into our stores or outdoor seating areas—even in states where 'open carry' is permitted—unless they are authorized law enforcement personnel."

Or finally, consider something that happened as I finished this book: ABC canceled the highly successful reboot of *Roseanne* one day after its star Roseanne Barr made a Twitter post that the network called "abhorrent, repugnant, and inconsistent with our values." In the past, a TV network might have waited to see how bad things got before acting. It might have simply released a statement condemning the views, compelled an apology from the star, maybe forced a sit-down between offended parties, and donated some money to support anti-racist causes. Instead, ABC took a projected loss of $60 million in revenue with this decision. They had a hit they could build around and even be proud of, as it represented disparate views in a polarized time (Roseanne's character was portrayed as a Trump supporter, as the actress is, while other characters, like her sister Jackie, were more left-of-center). That certainly raises their Hero Intensity, and clearly their Operational Excellence. But when ABC felt Barr crossed over from conservative to crazy, they acted.

Yes, the argument could be made that ABC never should have hired Barr back in the first place, since her history of tweeting out racist comments and conspiracy theories was well-known. But this is not like the story of the scorpion and the frog. Barr has always skated on the edge of what was appropriate, even when her first show was a hit for the network back in the 1980s and '90s, and they found a way to succeed. Sure, in the age of social media, there were risks something like this could go viral. But ABC rightly believed this show could represent all points of view and still be a hit if Roseanne stuck to the script. When she didn't, and ABC felt it had had enough, it acted. There's Hero Intensity in all parts of that story when it comes to values, along with Operational Excellence. Yet note I said Hero Intensity, not hero company. Like Dalio with his radical transparency, none of these things necessarily makes these companies heroes, just willing or learning to stand up for what they believe in. Once ABC made the decision, it cost them Operational Excellence in the short term but raised their Hero Intensity at the same time. What it does long term for both will be determined by whether the upcoming reboot for the show minus the star (*The Conners*) succeeds and how they handle future challenges to their convictions, which is as key to courage as having it in the first place.

So what are your non-negotiables?

BE A HERO: WRITE AND TEST YOUR NON-NEGOTIABLE VALUES

What are you non-negotiable on? What are the things you believe you will never change, the things you would look at yourself in the mirror and your people in the eye and say: "Listen, if you can't do this, you're out of here. I'm going to stand by this until the very end"?

▼ Write those out now.

▼ Then think about specific examples of how you have stood behind them—or failed to—when they were challenged and what happened.

▼ Now have your people repeat the first two steps and discuss what you get.

To help you think about this further, I asked some Hero Club members to talk about what having non-negotiable values meant to them:

▼ Dr. Rachel MK Headley, founder and senior partner of Rose Group International: "We have a set of core values that we hold ourselves to, we hold our clients to, and we hold our staff to. Our goal is to improve the energy of companies to increase success, so we focus on the culture, the internal experience of companies, and our philanthropy. Those are non-negotiable for us, so if there's ever a time when we're feeling like the clients don't buy it or our people don't buy it, then we're working with the wrong people or we need to change and refocus on those values. So for us, that's providing the highest value to our clients, our communities, and our people."

▼ Bill Wallace, founder of networking group Success North Dallas: "My noncompromises are integrity, servant leadership, and questioning. I want to be questioned; I want my people to question not only each other, but themselves. Because I have incredible, incredible growth out of that. We learned that from a family business we work with who wanted to be that way and turned that around on ourselves internally to create a culture of questioning, questioning ourselves and questioning each other: Did what we did add something? What happened? What were the results?"

▼ Rory Kelly, owner of Verizon retail chain CellOnly: "We have a golden rule in our company that you're not allowed to say no without permission. Most people expect 'no' when they walk in the door, especially when it comes to customer service. I own some Verizon Wireless stores, and in that retail environment, 'no' is just something kids have become accustomed to saying to people, and we had to change that. We just think 'no' is a lazy answer and prevents us from being truly dynamic."

▼ Christopher Cumby, founder of multimedia and sales consulting company Think Bold, Be Bold Ventures: "Honesty, being completely, brutally honest. I've found that it increased every relationship that I've ever had, because there's a lot of times where I'd hold back the honest truth of what I felt, or what I thought, and it cost me. It's OK to voice things from that perspective because it also gives me perspective and allows me to listen."

▼ Rob Beyer, president and CEO of EarthBend: "I've been publicly traded for most of my career and now I'm privately held, but the key is the same: consistency. If you share something a year ago and now all of a sudden you don't, that's when people get all bent out of shape. Everybody wants to work in an organization that's honest, right? You're honest, and you're upfront with folks. But I think the key is when you set your goals, get the focus, get the alignment, do all that stuff, and then you report against those goals, whether or not you're opening up your books, you just need to be consistent."

▼ Dave Newmark, cofounder of Newmark Advertising and CEO of online podcast directory PodSearch Inc.: "Do not lie. Ever,

ever, ever. Especially to yourself. Lies to staff or customers are obviously self-destructing. But lying to oneself is less obvious and can hurt even more deeply than lying to others. In 2005, I started a company that took off like a rocket; over 100 percent year-over-year growth. Then the 2008-09 recession hit, and things slowly began to go the other way. I saw the numbers but told everyone around me and myself that things would turn around. Essentially, I was lying to myself. Ultimately, we were able to sell the assets of the company and didn't get hurt too badly, but it was a hard and important lesson to always, always, always tell the truth. It's been good for my new business and great for my soul."

▼ Brigham Dickinson, president and founder of Power Selling Pros: "Think long and hard about your commitments. Once made, follow through. Unfulfilled commitments will always hurt the offender the most in the long run. Connect with every member on your team on an emotional level. Know who they are. What they like to do for fun. Periodically call them just because."

Got that? Agree? Disagree? That's not the point. The point is to know your core values exist and are being lived so you can test and define what is non-negotiable for you—where the core of your Hero Intensity duty lies. That doesn't mean you're going to be perfect. Bad hires, bad decisions, bad data, going against your gut . . . Anybody can make a mistake, freak out, or temporarily lose sight of who they are. Big mistakes (like getting stuck in your story and missing systemic failures) or small ones (like failing to serve a customer, then failing to make it right, and receiving a fair but stinging online rebuke)—we've all been there.

There are days I'm doing stuff for the C-Suite Network, and I'll see something that is not quite right and say, "Ah, let it go." But I have to stop myself before I start lying to myself and lose sight of my values. I have to say, "No. I can't let that go. That's not the quality we want. It's not reflective of our brand, and therefore it's not good enough.

That's going to cause me problems. It's going to make me lose money. I'm stopping it until we get it right."

That's what being right *operationally* is about. It's a little different when it comes to your values overall. Expecting close to perfection and having absolutes when it comes to every single value—100 percent compliance, no exceptions by your people and anyone you connect to—is almost as dangerous as having no values at all. You can't expect anybody's values to be perfect for you, except your own, and you can't let pride under the guise of living your values blind you to things that need to change. It shuts you down to different perspectives, new ways of thinking, and opportunities that you can't yet see—but someone else can.

FALLING ON YOUR "VALUES SWORD": NO ONE WILL BE ANYONE ELSE'S PERFECT

I'm sure some of you got your back up when I mentioned Chick-fil-A earlier because of the company's stand on gay rights and gay marriage, which has caused entire cities, like Boston, to reject the stores. The company's stand may be opposite to mine, and I hope it will change. But I still eat at the restaurants, and so do many gay people I know, who also hope for change. Does that mean they lack the courage of their convictions, in patronizing a business that does not support who they are and how they want to live? Actually, it's the opposite: They have the courage to support those who disagree. They still get served, no matter who they are, and made a choice to eat a delicious chicken sandwich, accepting that disagreement on values does not mean they cannot be civil (and full).

I respect that we can have different values and still break bread. I can still learn from and respect other things the company does: how they live their values, treat their people, and help their communities. Why do I have hope that even when it comes to seemingly non-negotiable values, things can and must change? Even Chick-fil-A makes exceptions to its closed-on-Sunday rule when that runs up against its need to give back to others: It will open in the case of emergencies to provide free food to those in need—as it did in Florida in 2016, following the shootings at a gay nightclub in Orlando.

> *No one is perfect.*
> *Even absolutes can be hard to come by when your*
> *non-negotiable values run into each other.*

To be honest, I only get my back up when people or organizations live by one rule, refuse to even consider that there could be exceptions, and then use that absolute to prevent you from accepting those who disagree (or who advocate any kind of violence against them).

I hope I'm not talking about you. Because all those people? They are convinced they have integrity and truth on their side and are living their values. On the face of it, non-negotiable values should only raise your Hero Intensity. But when they are used to exclude others, not because of any offenses against others or trespasses against you but because the way they look, think, or believe just offends you? That's being righteous under the guise of being right, a zealot not acting with zeal. Remember: ABC put *Roseanne* on the air knowing its star's views ran contrary to many at the network. When it cut ties, it was because what she did crossed a line. But ABC is owned by Disney, a purely capitalist company. Make no buts about it: The network had to have calculated that the long-term costs of keeping her show on the air outweighed the short-term hit of losing the client. (In Chapter 4, you learned Tom Landry of Allegiance Staffing did the same thing when he fired Igloo coolers as a customer.)

The nature of right and wrong is that values can evolve, and those values—even your non-negotiables—must be put to the test so you can understand that. What this means is you must have people opposing you—whether it's people who don't like what you stand for or companies who want to bring you down by doing what you do better or disrupting how you do it. Otherwise, it really isn't about you, right? Because you're not a big enough hero for your values to matter.

The question is, does that challenge cause you to open up or double down? And do you know the difference? Because there is no one way, no absolute right way, no matter how non-negotiable you are. A hero always needs a villain. Villains help heroes stand up for what they believe, test what they believe, and understand the complexities of doing the right thing. Being a hero is always about "doing the right thing." But what happens next?

Do you use what your "villains" are doing to turn the spotlight of accountability on yourself or just condemn their values?

What is right when it comes to values is rarely black and white, especially when the choices are not simple or the problem is one you have never encountered before. Operationally, "right" can be a little easier. It can be about being efficient and doing things the best way possible, as quickly as possible, using the fewest number of people without screwing those people and hurting those who most need our protection. In that way, doing something best and right might cost you. If you want to hire people from your community, it will cost you more than paying someone in Latin America or Southeast Asia.

When it comes to Hero Intensity, however, and being true to who you are, what you are, and what your values are, hero leadership can be messy. Complicated. Just like heroes in the comics are flawed, so is every leader, especially when perceived through the lens of others. So how do you deal with this messiness?

First and foremost, you do it by having the courage to be authentic. Always live your values, even if others don't like them or they seem stuck in the past:

▼ Say no if it doesn't fit into your values.
▼ Stay relentless even when the naysayers attack and the winds of change blow in the market.
▼ Do whatever it takes to lead and reach beyond what you know.
▼ Don't play politics or live with hidden agendas, but stand up and say what you believe.

Second, you do it by having the courage to evolve and change when necessary. I am the same person all the time. I do not care what people think about me, and I act the same around everyone. But that does not mean my values have always been the same. I've written about my non-negotiable values in my previous books, so I won't bore you with rehashing them here. I will say that today, I find I value relevance and significance more than ever—the knowledge that what I'm doing is, in some meaningful way, making a profound difference, especially for my children and grandchildren. In other words, I've evolved who I am and what I believe. I haven't left my previous values behind, but I have learned that evolution does not necessarily mean compromising those values, my Hero Intensity, or my Operational Excellence.

It's not compromising your authenticity or your Hero Factor to, well, compromise. Or at the very least to think differently about many of your core values—just not the non-negotiable ones. Which is where we go next in the final chapter in this part of our journey.

CHAPTER 9

COMPROMISE VS. EVOLUTION

In June 2015, the Supreme Court struck down state bans against gay marriage and legalized it nationwide. Prior to that ruling, gay marriage was already legal in many states, including . . . Idaho. *Idaho?* Not to slight anyone in Idaho, but in 2015, it was one of the ten most conservative states in the union, according to *Business Insider*. Yet gay marriage was not only legal in Idaho before it was the law of the land across the nation, but the majority of the state's residents supported it as well. It seems that Idahoans and their elected officials for the most part understood that not everyone needs to be like you, believe like you, or look like you to share your values, goals, and vision. And sometimes, when you realize that, values can change—or, rather, your views on them can evolve. Even on issues that deeply divide us.

Simply put, inclusion of independent and individual rights does not in and of itself undermine government or those citizens who believe differently—and it certainly won't undermine hero leaders and organizations. This is an important part of creating great, inclusive business cultures that value others and give back, and it starts with *really questioning* how you've done things and your values—either to make them better or evolve them into something new. If you do it genuinely and thoughtfully and not as an act of desperation to survive, win, or manipulate, the result is usually good. It might be uncomfortable and require much debate, but that's how you know what you're doing is essential for maintaining and growing your Hero Factor—just like it has been for our country.

The U.S. Constitution is a brilliant document. It defines our laws and what we value above all else. But our Founding Fathers knew what they wrote was not perfect and would need to be amended as the country got older and times changed. Most of us think of these amendments as coming decades and centuries after the Constitution was written, especially when it comes to valuing people (abolishing slavery) and individual rights (voting). But lest we forget, our "Bill of Rights" is in fact the first ten amendments. They were *not* part of the original document and were proposed six months and ratified two years after the Constitution was adopted.

If our Founding Fathers could amend our country's basic governing values after only a few months, what have you got to lose?

It's a disruptive time out there in business right now, and the change is best described as "violent." You can retrench, or you can push back—pick a side! America's belief in free enterprise and its entrepreneurial spirit hang in the balance. Heroes will lead the way, but it is prudent to recall Joseph Campbell's hero's journey here, or what he calls the "monomyth"—the journey taken by all people who become heroes. Like the Dog Soldiers, Campbell's heroes of myth start out ordinary, untested. They then battle fabulous forces and win, bestowing power and protection on their fellow men. They are more than good now. They are heroes through the courage they display. But what happens in the ultimate step in Campbell's hero journey? Heroes face their final battles with death (think Luke facing Darth Vader, Harry Potter facing Voldemort). True heroes win and return home with new knowledge—as Masters of Two Worlds.

So it will be in your business hero journey. You may have succeeded by innovating and instituting new beliefs and business practices for your service or product. You may have even created something completely new. You may have written and lived your values for a generation or more. But the real struggle comes over time—the battle for all you do to remain relevant and useful. What happens if you find you aren't simply stuck in your story but that your story is out of print? Do you have the courage to adapt? Do you go out while your Hero Factor is still high? Or do you get on your high horse and refuse to listen or compromise? You will lose your battle with death and the knowledge that comes with it—you will fail to master two worlds: the present and the future.

Many of us know the line from Proverbs in the Bible, even those who have never read the Bible: *Pride goeth before destruction, and a haughty spirit before a fall.* An important warning for our last stop on this part of our values journey.

As I said before, fear is a reaction; the courage to be a hero is a choice. What are you afraid of? Is it change? What do you think will happen if you question what you believe and how it is expressed in what you do and how you value others? Are you afraid it will cost you your status—your job—so you keep others out? That's playing the victim and living in some nostalgic and exclusionary version of the past. You think the best way forward is to keep those who threaten what you think of yourself, the way you think, or what you believe *out*?

Your Hero Factor is not compromised—just like Idaho's conservative bona fides or our Constitution—if you genuinely *evolve* your thinking and make what you do and how you act more expansive, less limiting, and less absolute. This is true for both sides of your Hero Factor: Operational Excellence and Hero Intensity.

SMELL THE FLOWERS: A STORY OF OPERATIONAL EXCELLENCE, HERO INTENSITY, AND EVOLUTION

Hello and welcome to Moviefone . . . If you know the name of the movie you want to see, press one now . . . Ring a bell, anyone? You picked up a phone, dialed 1-800-777-FILM, and the deep voice of Mr. Moviefone (Russ Leatherman) offered you access to all the movie times in your area. If you do remember this, you're probably over the age of 35 or have a deep love of 1990s nostalgia. You don't use a voice-activated phone system today to find what time and where the latest Marvel movie is playing . . . Oh, wait, you do. *OK, Google, what time is the Avengers movie playing?* What you don't need is to dial a phone number. Heck, I'm not sure how many Millennials even understand what an 800 number is. Who pays for long distance anymore?

So what if your business name is actually a 1-800 number? How do you evolve your Operational Excellence and grow when the origin of your name is irrelevant to most of your customers under the age of 35? Welcome to 1-800-Flowers.com, which started as brick-and-mortar retail stores in the 1970s, adopted the 800 number as the ultimate sales tool and its brand name in the 1980s, adapted from there into a leading provider of gifts for all occasions through its brands including Harry & David and The Popcorn Factory, and continued to evolve right up to 2018, when CEO Chris McCann won a "Visionary of the Year" award from VentureFuel for, among other things, the company's AI-powered online gift concierge, Gwyn, which is built on IBM's Watson platform.

"Gwyn and all of what we are doing around that is all part of what we call the fifth wave of change for us," says McCann. Five waves since 1976? That's evolving your Operational Excellence.

McCann's brother Jim started in the flower business in 1976, when Chris was still in high school and "had no choice but to work for him." Chris calls those early years his "indentured servant days that I'm still trying to get paid for," but he still joined the business full time in 1984, when his brother had grown it to 12 stores. He needed to, because his brother was only there part time; Jim had a full-time job as a social worker. "According to Jim, shortly after that, he put me in charge of the 12 stores and then, the next thing he knew, we had . . . three," Chris says. "Which is true, but usually he leaves out the fact that we were doing more business and certainly more profit out of those three than we were out of the 12."

Chris had seen the potential in consolidation, but he was also eyeing 1-800 toll-free service. 800 numbers had been around since the 1960s but became affordable and prolific following the breakup of the AT&T monopoly in the early 1980s, which caused rates to fall. The McCanns managed to acquire the 1-800-Flowers number in 1986, just as companies really started to adopt the service, and it changed consumer behavior. "Our customers got much more comfortable coming to us on the telephone and having their product delivered than they were having to walk into the stores," says Chris. "We did some traffic analysis on the stores and realized it was costing us more to open the front door every day than [we were making from] business coming in through the front door. We changed our model and embraced the second wave of growth for our company, which was telephonic commerce."

They did more than that. In the late 1980s and early '90s, the company branded itself around a telephone number and really disrupted the floral industry: It became one of the first national companies to use its number 24/7.

This is the point where too many companies' stories fall apart when it comes to Operational Excellence: They fail to adapt while they are successful and lose their Hero Factor, or even their entire business. 1-800-Flowers.com did not. It started its third wave of change even before the second wave crashed: online services. Says Chris: "We didn't know much about it and really what it would be, other than that if consumers embraced this like they had 800 service, someone else could disrupt us. So we decided we'd better get involved early and learn what this new technology is."

The company launched its first store on CompuServe in 1991 and became the first company to sell any product of any kind on AOL in 1994. It just kept riding the wave of ecommerce until the mid-2000s and its fourth wave: mobile communications and social media. That brings us to the company's fifth wave, taking place today. "In 2016, we saw a confluence of technologies starting to take shape that could change consumer behavior: 'conversational commerce,'" Chris says. "It's the confluence of big data, analytics, and predictive analytics, AI, and voice as the primary user interface. We launched a bot on Facebook Messenger. Two weeks later, we launched a skill on Amazon's Alexa platform. Two weeks after that, we launched Gwyn, an AI-powered gift concierge utilizing the Watson platform. In 2018, we launched on Google Assistant and Apple's Business Chat. So clearly, the consumer adoption into that mode of voice communication is taking place."

So 1-800-Flowers.com is at the forefront of technology once again, having come almost full circle—something that is not lost on Chris: "We kind of think it's ironic that a company that maintained its branding around a phone number that doesn't mean anything to anyone anymore is back to voice as the primary mode of interaction," he says.

Chris's focus is also back on people, both customers and employees—where Operational Excellence and Hero Intensity must intersect both internally and externally. You may not have or need as many "operators standing by," but you still need a human side. As we move our focus from having values to valuing others in determining your Hero Intensity, you cannot allow your evolving Operational Excellence to leave your Hero Intensity behind, unless you want to become a Bottom Liner.

This is exactly what tech companies that ostensibly want to make our world a better, more connected place *should* get but don't—they pass themselves off as Heroes when they are really just Bottom Liners. There has been a raft of stories about how disillusioned people are working in tech, especially in Silicon Valley. It's not just the misogyny or lack of diversity; it's the people who came in with a desire to create a better tomorrow and discovered that all their company wants to do is monetize everything they possibly can. This is what happened with Facebook, when it allowed Cambridge Analytica to mine its users' personal information and use it to potentially influence elections. Facebook initially denied the charge, then said it didn't do anything wrong, anything they didn't have a right to do, and anything you did not allow them to do. It has since faced fines in the United Kingdom and is under investigation by other governments. The point isn't whether you believe them or not but that there was no transparency, no sense of what it would cost its users, no belief in anything but the bottom line. That doesn't make you evil. It just doesn't make you a hero who values your customers, and that will cost you in the end no matter how big you are.

> *Hero companies and leaders know as you evolve your Operational Excellence, you need to equally evolve your Hero Intensity to stay in balance.*

Simply put, the point of evolving your Operational Excellence cannot be to remove the need for relationships with your people and your customers. On the contrary, if you're able to be more productive and grow with fewer people, you need to pay *more* attention to those people—and your customers, all of whom wield the power of Twitter and online reviews. You should never compromise your values for a customer, but you need to value them if you expect them to value you.

In my opinion, this is where hero businesses that work in brick-and-mortar retail or have experience in it even if they have evolved beyond it like 1-800-Flowers.com can have a distinct advantage. As long as they don't cling to the way things used to be.

"We often refer back to the very first flower shop we had on the Upper East Side in Manhattan," Chris says. "We talk about the interactions we had, knowing the people, knowing their different styles, where they could pop in the store and say, 'Hey, I need an arrangement for my wife. I'll be back later to pick it up.' We knew what they wanted, what their tastes were, what the wife liked. You could really have that one-to-one relationship, a belief my brother brought to the business from his days as a social worker. He believed if you want to really connect with someone, you need to build a relationship with them first. Build relationships first, do business second. We maintained that when we embraced telephonic commerce. Today we ask, 'How can we use technology to scale but still maintain that kind of relationship?'"

The answer is a lesson for all businesses: Put the customer in charge of your brand. Since you can't touch every customer every day the way you used to, let consumers use their ecommerce, mobile, social

---

BE A HERO: EVOLVE YOUR VALUES

Think you can't evolve on your deepest values and still survive? Even one of the most conservative states in the nation, Alabama, understands the nature of changing values. One of its favorite sons, former Governor George Wallace, famously declared "Segregation now, segregation tomorrow, segregation forever" in 1963, renounced it by 1972, and actually became more popular afterward. You may not have grown up in a segregated South, but every business has faced some challenge to the way they do things: Dress codes, flexible work hours, customer service approaches, company benefits . . . leaders and organizations have evolved their stances on many things. If they haven't, chances are they are Wannabes—or, worse, dead.

Simply put, *what* we have evolved our stance on doesn't necessarily tell us *why* and what that change says about our values. Ask yourself and your team the following questions:

▼ What have you evolved your stance on? What have you refused to evolve your stance on?

▼ What do your answers say about what you value? Do they reaffirm your values, show that your values have changed, or broaden the definition of those values and what non-negotiable means to you?

---

media, and conversational commerce to engage with your brand and open it up to them. Make them feel important. Give them influence. That's how you, as Chris puts it, "provide one-to-one personal relationships at scale."

But don't stop there. You need to allow your people to have influence, too. Sometimes we forget that valuing integrity is not just about what *you* do and how *you* think but allowing *others* to think and act with integrity, too.

EVOLVE YOUR THINKING

So what's your strategy for evolution? What's your plan to do more than the same thing again and again, just packaged differently? Or as Glenn Llopis puts it in *The Innovation Mentality*, "Without strategy, change is merely substitution, not evolution. America may be innovative in many things, but . . . too many businesses and leaders have stopped reinventing themselves and have instead remained complacent for decades, only to find themselves unprepared for real evolution."

In other words, we get stuck not in the story of our values but in our thinking that we have changed or evolved, when we have just put lipstick on the same old pig. Gotten trapped in our past and our old ways of doing things. Stuck in old beliefs, self-imposed limitations, and reasons "why not." That's not going to give you Hero Intensity today, even if it did yesterday. That's not a fight for a better tomorrow. That's checking a box, not thinking big to act bigger!

Erik Anderson, executive chairman of Topgolf Entertainment Group, calls this evolution "intellectual integrity" and has grown his business by allowing it to evolve beyond best practices to best thinking: "It's the best thinking that's more important than the best practice," he says. "Best practice sounds like I have to break away from something. Best thinking is core. When that's happening all the time, in little things and big things, the organization becomes a learning organization, a learning organism, that's constantly going toward the best information. People understand that's an organization of intellectual integrity."

So what does that mean in operational terms? It means you think bigger and beyond the bottom line. "We measure value creation over ten years," adds Anderson. "If I miss the 'B' word, budget, this year by $500,000, but learn something that allows me to earn $200,000 a year for the next ten years, which organization do you want to be with? The one that missed $200,000 a year for ten because it measures to budget, or the one that said, 'I'm going to take the budget hit, bad news, made a mistake, but I learned $2 million.' That person who changed the arc of the company and learned is enormously valuable. Because you've changed the whole progress of the company, you've changed the entire direction. That's what happens with model thinking, and when you tell everybody, 'Please tell me how this works over the next ten years, not to the next quarter.'"

That's what it's like for heroes and values. Values get stretched. Values get tested. As I learn, listen to understand, question to become enlightened, and gain experience, my values don't change—they evolve. They evolve because I choose to let them. Because I can. Because it's good for me, good for the business, and *good for others*.

PART II HERO CHECK
QUESTIONS ON YOUR VALUES

As you move forward into Part III about how you value others, reconsider these questions about your values that we covered in Part II: living them, testing them, standing up for them, and knowing when they might need to evolve.

- ▼ Are your values clearly stated for everyone—your people, partners, vendors, customers, clients, members, and community—to see?

- ▼ Does everyone you work with know what your values are? Have you asked them?

- ▼ Does what you say your values are align with what your people think—and what your *customers and clients* think—your values are and with your actions?

- ▼ How are your people living your values?

- ▼ How do you avoid getting stuck in your story? Do you review your values regularly, testing that they are being lived?

▼ Do you have the courage of your convictions and stand up for the values you feel you cannot compromise?

▼ What values are non-negotiable for you, and what are you willing to compromise or sacrifice for the greater good or changing times?

▼ Do you have the courage to stand up for—and reconsider—your non-negotiable values when they are challenged and when new thinking emerges?

▼ When was the last time you updated your values? Or do you see them all as fixed points?

▼ Have you evolved what you believe and thus evolved your values?

PART III

HERO INTENSITY
HOW YOU VALUE OTHERS

Now that your values are in place, it's time to make their impact as expansive as possible. The first part of building your Hero Intensity is creating, understanding, testing, and evolving your values when it comes to your company and leadership. The second part is doing the same thing in how you value others: being accountable to, empowering, and giving back to others, not simply yourself and your bottom line. By "others," I mean the people you connect to and the world you live in—your relationships with the people who work with and for you, as well as your customers, partners, community, and the environment. By "giving back," I mean to all your people (bottom to top) and giving the things you and they care about beyond 10 percent of all net profits of a product or service going to charity. This "other directedness" is something you feel as much as you measure. But remember: If your Hero Intensity drops because you fail to value others, your Operational Excellence will suffer, and your Hero Factor will decline, if not plummet.

CHAPTER 10

THE FEEL OF A CULTURE THAT VALUES OTHERS

I had known Nido Qubein for decades as a businessman and through the National Speakers Association before he became the seventh president of High Point University in North Carolina in 2005. Before he assumed the post, High Point was not exactly failing, but it was hardly thriving. It was stuck, barely breathing. Most disconcertingly, it was losing its relevance among its customers (students), people and community (faculty and administrators), and donors. With an enrollment of 1,450 students, 108 full-time faculty, a 91-acre campus that housed 22 buildings, and an operating budget of $38 million, you would be forgiven for thinking High Point's better days were behind it. After all, colleges and universities are notoriously slow to adapt and change—even when faced with mirror moments that reveal they are on their last legs.

But where others saw an organization in decline, Nido saw opportunity, possibility, and a place ready to live by a new entrepreneurial mission: "marching onwards with faithful courage." That courage—the same courage we covered in the last part—has taken High Point far. In 2017, the university had an enrollment of 4,500 students, 300 full-time faculty, a 430-acre campus that housed 112 buildings, and an operating budget of $290 million. It has been named one of the best regional colleges in the South. It is building a new basketball arena and even has a steakhouse on campus, a fact that makes me want to go back to school there.

All this is stunning considering most of that growth happened during the Great Recession. That was not what impressed me most, however, when I visited Nido at High Point; it was a candy wrapper. I was getting a tour from Nido and some of his staff, and as we crossed the campus, one of his vice presidents casually bent down, picked up a candy wrapper, and stuck it in his pocket. I don't think he even noticed that I saw him do it. Because he wasn't doing it for me. He was doing it because he wanted to. He was doing it because he cared.

At this point, you might be saying: *Really, Jeff? A candy wrapper? That's your opening culture story?* Yes. Yes, it is. What? You expected a story with big numbers and bold actions accounting for millions of dollars and impacting thousands of people? Well, that's in the High Point story, too. But what do those numbers actually tell you beyond the bottom line? It's the small stories of individual responsibility and accountability that inspire me and demonstrate cultures that have true Hero Intensity. These stories are powerful statements about what your values are and how they are being lived. They speak volumes about how you value others and how they, in turn, value your leadership and organization.

That gentleman who casually picked up a candy wrapper while walking across campus reminded me of the man tossing a beached starfish back in the ocean in the story "The Star Thrower" by Loren Eiseley. The narrator who comes across the man is initially baffled by his actions. He cannot possibly hope to save all the starfish in the world and hold off death. He leaves but later realizes the man wasn't doing it to be noticed or rewarded, and he didn't think he could save all the starfish. He was doing it simply because he cared about something more than himself—about the life of each starfish on that beach. The narrator returns the next day, moved by the man's actions, understanding that he had been "unbelieving, hardened by the indifference of maturity." He becomes a star thrower himself, knowing "after us there will be others."

Like the star thrower, the person picking up the candy wrapper wasn't doing it to impress me. He was doing it because he was one of those inspired by Nido's leadership and the culture at High Point. He was one of Nido's star throwers. He picked up the candy wrapper because *that's what he did*. Because he *felt* he should.

HERO CULTURES ARE FELT, NOT JUST SEEN

In *Jacobellis v. Ohio*, the 1964 U.S. Supreme Court case about what constitutes "obscene material," Justice Potter Stewart wrote in his opinion, "I shall not today attempt further to define the kinds of material I understand to be embraced within that shorthand description; and perhaps I could never succeed in intelligibly doing so. But I know it when I see it." That's very similar to how I feel about hero cultures. But culture is more than what you see. It is also the *feeling* you get at the same time. So with apologies to Justice Potter: "I shall not today attempt further to define the kinds of **hero culture** I understand to be embraced within that shorthand description; and perhaps I could never succeed in intelligibly doing so. But I know it when I **feel** it."

Hero or Zero, Bottom Liner or Struggling Do-Gooder, or anywhere in between, you feel the culture of a company—or, more

> *Do you see* **and** *feel your values being lived*
> *by your people in the culture of your organization?*

precisely, how the people *make* it feel, individually and as part of a team. Don't tell me you don't feel that Hero Intensity in a company that has it—and that it doesn't matter. This feeling runs deeper than what we call "mood." It speaks to how an organization's core values serve and respect others. Companies that have hero cultures also have teams ready to disrupt and challenge the status quo. They are more than just great places to work—they're places where people can't wait to go to sleep so they can get up and go back to work the next day. I felt that energy at High Point, not only in the candy wrappers that got picked up that day but also in the ways the people on campus lived. I saw people from students to faculty to Nido himself hold doors open for others. That's a sign people are taking individual responsibility in a culture that values other people. That screams service and fellowship to me. That screams, "I take pride in being here and living these values."

You can't impose a culture like that; you have to live and develop it over time. It is not something one action reveals or one proclamation can create (though as we have seen and will see again, it *is* something one bad action can undo—at least temporarily). Nido couldn't just say one day, "Hey, we're going to be an entrepreneurial university," implement a variation on the same way the university had been conducting business, and then sit back and wait for improvement. That's lipstick on a pig. That's selling a story and hoping everyone doesn't notice when you don't actually adapt or evolve. That's not a hero culture in the way you see *or* feel the values of the company being lived.

Culture is the cumulative effect of *all* the people in the business working together, based on your and their values, operating with one another over time to deliver results. This can be hard to measure. After all, how do you measure a feeling? Feelings are entirely subjective, and their expression varies from person to person. Just because I'm yelling doesn't mean I'm angry. Just because you don't laugh doesn't mean you don't find my jokes funny. Which they are.

Which is also my point. Culture isn't right or wrong: It's heroic or not. It may feel right to you, but that doesn't necessarily make you a hero to anyone but yourself and your bottom line. If you're a Bottom Liner maintaining high Operational Excellence, that's not wrong.

It just isn't heroic, because you aren't balancing that Operational Excellence with Hero Intensity.

Culture is also about growth—it *has* to be, as with High Point and the stories that follow. But growth in what direction: toward the Bottom Liner side or the Hero side? It's your choice: Pick a side! Start by answering these questions:

> ▼ Does your organization value people and profit in balance?
> ▼ Do you want this part of your Hero Intensity—how you value others—to matter as much as making the sale?
> ▼ Do your leaders live that value?
> ▼ Does your company stand up for others even in hard times?
> ▼ Do you value and include ALL people when living your values?
> ▼ Are you giving back to your people, community, and beyond in a way that matters to them, rather than pats you on the back for your generosity?

Answer any of these questions with anything less than a "mostly yes," and your culture is definitely lacking in Hero Intensity. That requires creating and sustaining a culture driven by decisive, confident-yet-vulnerable, inclusive leaders who value everyone who shares the goals of the company and delivers results—even those whom they personally disagree with or who look, speak, believe, or work differently than they do or the way things "have always been done." Fail to do that, and your people, partners, and customers will fast lose trust in you, and you will become irrelevant to all but those who value exactly what you value. Then you will retain only the people and customers who see your benefit as purely transactional—or in other words, good for *their* bottom line.

The effect of this Hero Intensity *is* measurable; its absence is just felt long before it shows up operationally, as your people do just enough to collect their paychecks—or get bullied by those who thrive in your toxic culture. They silo, protect their turf, and refuse to do more than what is asked of them. Eventually opportunities and possibilities don't just get ignored—no one looks for them in the first place. Innovation dries up. No one smiles on their way to work. No one cares about anything but themselves because the culture doesn't value that.

No one cares about candy wrappers on the ground or starfish on the beach.

THE HUMAN FACTOR AND THE HERO FACTOR

One day while on the road I called a Lyft to get to my next meeting, and a young man about 23 years old picked me up. We got to chatting. He was an aspiring musician, but music didn't pay all the bills, so he had been working as a sales manager at an auto parts store and driving for Lyft in his spare time. But he said he had recently left the auto parts job. I asked him why, and he told me that no one there cared about anyone else. They simply yelled at the employees, treated the customers like a necessary evil, and turned every mistake into a capital crime. "It was so bad," he said, "that by the end I was paying people to finish my shift rather than do it myself."

Question: What does it take to make a culture that bad?

Answer: Be a Zero and forget that we are all human—and then treat your people, customers, partners, and neighbors as commodities to buy, sell, and replenish. As a means to your financial ends, no matter how morally corrupt or bankrupt or devoid of kindness and goodness that may be.

Treating people as disposable or necessary evils you must endure until the robots take all our jobs is not how you get Operational Excellence. It is worth noting that Elon Musk, the man who tried to automate as much of his business as possible to create driverless cars and replace humans everywhere, admitted in 2018 he relied on too many robots and undervalued humans at Tesla. Attributing recent safety problems, injuries, defects, and delays to the company's excessive drive to automate, Musk decided to fire some of those robots in favor of human workers. As he said on Twitter: "Yes, excessive automation at Tesla was a mistake. To be precise, my mistake. Humans are underrated."

> *How do you feel your values being lived every day in the mood and actions of your people who work for and with you?*

I admire Musk's willingness to admit his mistake—something many in the tech world are doing recently (i.e., apologizing). But I would say that Musk did more than underrate humans. He *undervalued* them. In fact, he might not have even been thinking about them at all. In a time when all people are looking to feel significant—to know that they matter—Musk's "mistake" was exchanging part of his Hero Intensity for what he thought would be Operational Excellence. He got neither. He did to his people exactly what traditional car manufacturers and other companies did to so many workers in the Rust Belt when they sent their jobs beyond our borders: traded them for something cheaper.

Yes, I said "something," not "someone." You aren't really considering people as people when you see them as commodities.

That extends to your customers as well. Too often companies and leaders don't see the link between workplace culture and how they treat their customers, clients, partners, and vendors. Valuing others to create a hero workplace means great people caring about the work they do—everything from customer service to accounting to inventory to IT and beyond. But if you see your people as commodities or transactional, the likelihood is they will see the people your company serves as commodities or transactions as well. Then you have a culture problem *and* a marketplace or "reputation management" problem that mea culpas, PR strategies, community service, and marketing initiatives can't entirely fix.

Every day organizations, leaders, and teams have to choose how they live their values: how to step into a meeting, how to run the meeting, how to interact with one another, how to treat customers, how to negotiate with vendors. You can choose to be an asshole, difficult, kind, or all those things and still value others in the process, even in the difficult times. Your people will notice when you do. For example, Pirooz Abir, CEO of LiquidInvoice LLC, told me he sold his previous business because he could not see eye to eye with his partner: "Employees came back and told me, 'We're heartbroken that you're leaving because you cared for the employees.' My employees felt that I was the connection between them and the ownership of the business. I'm glad to have left that legacy behind, and I'm hearing from them now as they found out I have a new startup. They're all calling me and asking, 'When can we come work with you?'"

Simply put, people are your greatest asset. Musk is doing now what Nido and High Point, as well as most hero companies, have been doing for much longer: focusing more "holistically" on the way he does business. That means always considering how you value others. As Nido told me on my *All Business* radio show, "We are focused

---

BE A HERO: HAVE AN EXIT INTERVIEW

Have your employees ever answered the question "What's the best part of this company?" with "the people" *in their exit interview*? That's a sure sign they are valuing each other, but the culture is not valuing them. Take a step back and try to understand how what you are doing affects the people around you. In other words, have the "exit interview" now.

▼ Make an appointment with the people who answer to you and ask them modified versions of the exit interview questions with the intent of getting them to stay!

▼ When you ask about the best and worst parts of the company, ask how the company culture supports or doesn't support that aspect, and how it could change for the better.

---

on assisting those who we seek to serve and interpret from their perspective. When you do that, people pay attention and want to help you. It's good to create for a purpose and have lofty goals, as long as you back them up with education and deliver on the promise."

Remember: Your brand is nothing more than a promise delivered. Your culture is an internal manifestation of how you project that brand to the world and the values behind it. Or, as my friend and Hero Club member Bill Wallace, founder of Success North Dallas, says, "Culture trumps all. Culture is your brand. When you mess with your culture, you mess with your brand."

That goes for better, as in the case of High Point, or for worse, as in the following stories, which show what happens when your culture doesn't care—or stops caring.

CHAPTER 11

CRASH LANDING
WHEN CULTURES
FAIL TO CARE

Dave Sanderson wasn't supposed to be on US Airways Flight 1549, which was scheduled to fly from LaGuardia Airport in New York City to Charlotte, North Carolina, on January 15, 2009. Dave was on the road for his job at a major software company at the time, and his work for a client in Brooklyn had started at 5:00 A.M. and finished early. He managed to switch from the late afternoon flight to the one before. It was a cold winter day in New York, as in 21 degrees cold. He was happy to be heading home.

At the gate, Dave used his preferred status to board early, settled into window seat 15A, and did what seasoned business travelers often do: put his briefcase down, pulled out something to read, and tuned everything out. Flight 1549 was cleared for takeoff just around 3:25 P.M. Two minutes after it left the ground, Dave heard the explosion. It was louder than anything he had heard on a plane before, and it immediately got his attention. He looked out his window and saw fire coming out from underneath the left wing. Still, Dave didn't panic. He knew sometimes planes lose engines and can still fly. Then he heard Captain Chesley "Sully" Sullenberger say these words as the plane crossed over the George Washington Bridge: "This is your captain. Brace for impact."

Now Dave knew it was serious. He started thinking about whether he would make it or not, but there wasn't time to think about it for long. About five minutes after it took off, Flight 1549 crash-landed in New York City's Hudson River.

It was a hard hit. Dave smashed back into his seat on impact, and as he came back up, he looked out the window. He saw light and felt a moment of relief. He knew he had a chance to live, but the plane was filling rapidly with water. Where he was, in the middle of the plane, the water was already knee deep. The back of the plane was waist deep. He needed to move forward. Thinking at first only of himself, his game plan became "get to the aisle, get up front, and get out."

But when he got to the aisle, he stopped. He heard his mother's voice in his head: "If you do the right thing, God will take care of you."

Dave knew what the right thing was: help others first. Instead of moving forward, he went back into his row, climbed over the seats to the back of the plane, and got behind everybody else making their way out. He was not going to leave until he was sure everyone else was off that plane. And when they were, Dave turned into the exit row and prepared to dive out onto the wing or into a lifeboat, like those before him had. But when he got to the door, there was no more room. So he stayed inside the plane and waited for rescuers to arrive.

The 36-degree water was waist deep now. He was cold, but as calm as he could be. He was alive, after all. Then, after about six or seven minutes, he felt the plane shift. Later Dave found out the movement was caused by a tugboat hitting the front of the plane, but at that moment, he thought, "I'm on the *Titanic*. I've got to get out of here. This thing's going down, man." He jumped into the river, swam to the closest boat, and held on to the outside.

That's where Dave was when he was rescued. He was taken to a New Jersey hospital and diagnosed with hypothermia. It took about five hours to warm him up. In those five hours, he met with the governor of New Jersey, the head of the Port Authority, the New York State Police, the New Jersey State Police, the FBI, Homeland Security, the media . . . Others on the flight had gone home, but Dave was trapped in the hospital and available for questioning.

He remained in the hospital overnight. US Airways sent him a personal liaison, and she took care of anything he needed until he was cleared to fly to Charlotte the next day. His family hadn't been able to get to New York, but the TSA let them meet him at the gate and have their tearful reunion away from the cameras, which were waiting in droves outside security. None of them were ready for the media onslaught, but they made it through. Afterward, Dave insisted on getting his car, even though his wife told him he shouldn't be driving. So she sent two of their kids to watch over him, which he admits was a smart move. Less smart was Dave's decision to stop at the office, but since it was on the way home, he decided to check in. He wanted them to know he was OK.

Not that they seemed to care. Neither Dave nor his wife had heard from anyone in the office. Maybe they didn't know he was in the crash? After all, he wasn't supposed to be on that flight. Was no one looking for one of their top-producing employees? Did no one watch the news?

Dave walked in, looking pale, still wearing the sweats the Red Cross had given him at the hospital, his kids by his side. He went to his office and announced to the team, "I just wanted to check in and let you know that I'm OK." Some people came up and gave him big hugs, and as they did, he saw his boss approaching. Dave smiled, and his boss said the words every person in Dave's situation would want to hear:

"Are you going to Michigan next week?"

HERO FAIL: FEELING LIKE A NUMBER

No one I tell that story to isn't shocked when I hit that line, especially when they find out the boss wasn't joking. It's one thing if Dave wasn't thinking clearly, as evidenced by his driving to the office. I can totally imagine an employee like Dave, who is in shock and cares about his job and the people he works with, saying to his boss, perhaps jokingly, "I'll still go to Michigan next week."

If that were my employee, I'd like to think I would say, after a proper hug, "Are you serious?" or "We can talk about that later. How are you?" OK, knowing me, it would probably be something like, "What the bleeping hell are you bleeping talking about?" Actually, that's not true. If I was anything close to a hero, I would never have even had the conversation, because I would have already tracked him down and arranged to take care of him, or at least spoken to his wife and made sure everything was OK at home.

Imagine you were Dave. What would you do? "At first, I wasn't putting things together," Dave says. "I was like, 'What do you mean?' and he goes, 'Well, we got a meeting in Michigan. You're going to Michigan next week, right?' And my kids are looking at me: 'Dad, what are you going to do?' And I said, 'Yeah, I'll go.' I wasn't thinking right."

Anyone thinking that Dave's manager was just a bad apple dealing with an extraordinary situation (focused on short-term potential revenue and not having to train a new associate instead of the long-term associate and the long-term revenue potential and potentially a raving fan in the client) should know this: A culture that allows a bad apple like that to rise through the ranks either does not care, is hostile, or is toxic. And eventually it does affect your Operational Excellence. You are only as strong as your weakest link, and your culture is defined by it. Even if your chain is strong now, its strength will be tested. And in all fairness, Dave said, his boss's boss later told him he didn't have to go, and if he "needed to take some time off, he could." But Dave, who was a man of his word, said, "No, I committed to go, so I'll go." He also wanted to put the exchange in perspective. It was 2009. The crash that led to the Great Recession was still being felt by every business, including his. "No one was buying software, and that's what I was in," Dave says. "I had one of the biggest transactions in the company going. So putting it from my boss's perspective, he has this big number he's looking at, and I'm the conduit to the number because I had the total relationship. So if something happened to me, something would happen to the transaction."

> *What has the higher value to you: the transaction or*
> *the people involved in that transaction?*

Note two of the words Dave uses here: *transaction* and *relationship*. Those two words fall on opposite sides of the Hero Factor:

▼ "Transaction" is about numbers, or Operational Excellence; you can't have revenue without transactions of some kind. You *can* have transactions without any kind of relationship, but the more you do, the more they are devoid of Hero Intensity.

▼ "Relationship" is about people and the values that drive your Hero Intensity; you can't value others if you don't have the desire to relate to them, let alone forge a relationship. You *can* have business relationships without a transaction, but if you're not getting as much as you're giving? That will cost you some Operational Excellence.

The key when considering Dave's story is the need for balance between transactions and relationships, especially in times of crisis. The software company Dave worked for *should* have been concerned about the deal. Those were tough times, and the deal probably meant as much to the company's bottom line as it did to Dave's. But how his company expressed that concern says everything about its culture and how they valued him—or, rather, didn't—beyond the bottom line. They weren't thinking about their relationship with Dave first—or even at all. They didn't value him. They valued the transaction. They cared about the numbers.

Which is exactly how Dave felt: "That conversation taught me something at that moment: I was just a number to my manager and possibly my company," he says. "What if I had died that day? I was very close. Things could have happened a lot of different ways. Not only the crash but drowning in the water and getting hypothermia. I thought, 'My boss would have had somebody in that seat the next day. Maybe I'm just a number to these people. Maybe they don't care about me.' I loved the company I was with. They had tremendous people. But that one interaction told me that I was just a number. And candidly, I wasn't living to my values that you take care of your people."

Those values lie in the words he remembered his mom saying as he jumped up to get out of the plane. They were values his company didn't have when it mattered most to Dave, or they or at least his direct manager weren't living them; otherwise, the culture would have been different. US Airways did have them, according to Dave, which did everything it could to make the best of a bad situation that was no fault of theirs and made sure he was always taken care of. So did his client in Michigan, which Dave says was "tremendous" and "unbelievable," doing everything his company failed to do: "They took care of my family. They gave us gifts. They flew me out to make sure that I was OK."

Dave sees this as a lesson in leadership—hero leadership, or in his company's case, Zero Hero Intensity. And it is. Attitude and actions reflect leadership, but leadership is a product of the culture that creates it, the values a company lives by, and how it values others—and how that translates into that company and leader's Hero Factor. How it makes your company and your people *feel*.

"The first thing you do when somebody goes down is you take care of whatever you have to operationally," Dave adds. "But more importantly, you take care of the person's family. And I think that was what hurt me more than anything else. I'm a big boy. I can handle it. But nobody even checked in on my wife. She was here all by herself. I told the HR people later that, if I could give them some coaching, the first thing you do is you call the spouse. Check in. See if there's anything you can do. You can make a raving fan out of one of your associates just by understanding the situation they're in. Taking care of them when they're down, when they have a challenging time. I am a raving fan for US Airways and now American for the rest of my life. I fly them almost exclusively. They got my business because they took care of me."

Dave and others know that when you have a culture that cares enough to do that, you don't just get employees who care back but who push to do more. They will follow you anywhere, because they know you have their backs. That feeling extends to the marketplace as well, and not just to your customers. Potential recruits and future talent notice, whether you move on (like Pirooz Abir in Chapter 10) or keep doing what you have been doing for decades. Tom Landry of Allegiance Staffing notes: "If you do the right thing a huge percentage of the time, you get a reputation. People notice. We just got called by a guy who said he had been following us for three or four *years*, and he really wanted to join our team. When people start seeking you out to be part of that, that's kind of confirmation that you're on the right track."

That's the ultimate proof that your values are being lived in the culture you create: When others want to come to you and stay with you because of who you are, not how much money you pay them. That's the difference between a Hero company and a Good Co. that values others or a Bottom Liner that values the bottom line:

▼ Hero companies take care of their people and make fans out of them very quickly. They may never leave, and they stay loyal fans even if they do.

▼ A Good Co. does the same but with less Hero Intensity—they make you feel good, not great, but still make you feel nothing less than valued.

▼ Bottom Liners treat people like they're just a number. It doesn't necessarily mean that they will leave, but they will never become your evangelists. And as soon as the opportunity arises, those people are usually gone.

Which is what happened to Dave Sanderson: He became a number to his leaders and company. So they became all about numbers to him—a means to an end.

WHEN THE NUMBERS STOP ADDING UP

Dave Sanderson was in a terrible position. That Michigan deal was one of the biggest transactions at his company. It meant a lot of money in a lousy economy. He knew soon after he said yes that if he had said no, his boss probably would have sent somebody else and Dave would have lost or at the very least had to split a seven-figure commission. I'll say it again, because it bears repeating: None of this makes the company evil, just far from being a Hero company. They were Bottom Liners pure and simple, and now, so was Dave. He stayed because they were a means to an end. Millions of dollars are a lot to lose. Dave didn't want to take the hit to his bottom line, either. After all, he had four kids to put through college. He just became even more about his Operational Excellence as an employee. He was already a top producer, and he dug into that role. While he never believed again that the company had his back, he still made sure he had the backs of his clients and the people who worked for him. The client at that Michigan meeting had asked for assurances that they would be supported if Dave left, because they felt they were a good fit with him, not necessarily his company. So he assured them he would stay, and he did. A little over two years later, he got promoted to a different division and responsibility but kept selling, generating tons of new business for the firm. But if his company expected that would add up to a lifetime of shared excellence, they were wrong. His relationship with them was now purely transactional.

> *Don't mistake compliance or complacency for commitment or a caring culture.*

The relationship between Dave and his company ended on the fifth anniversary of the crash of Flight 1549, which brought up all the feelings he had had back in 2009. He told the company how he felt as he left for New York City. He told them where they could see him on national TV. And . . . nothing. No one called to see how it went or how he felt. No one called his wife to say they had seen him on TV and was she OK? No one found a way to right a wrong and care enough to, well, care.

Dave left that software company soon after and founded his own business to help companies avoid the same mistakes and do better—to care about and value others. He speaks on leadership across the country, but despite the acclaim he has received it wasn't until years later that his old company asked him back to speak to them—outta sight, outta mind. "I could have been their biggest ombudsman around the world," Dave notes. "But they never even thought about me. They lose a lot of great people and business because of that lack of a relationship—relationships I still have with others. Today, I still interact with my former clients, and they look at me not only as their former sales guy but as a friend and as a confidant, where I give them

---

BE A HERO: HAVE A CULTURAL MIRROR MOMENT

Thinking about Dave's story, look yourself in the mirror and ask yourself these questions. Keep the answers in mind when it comes to assessing your Hero Intensity:

▼ Think about a time you showed you cared about others more than cash—that you put people over profit, because it was the right thing to do. How did it make you feel? How did it make your people feel? What did you or they wish you had done differently? What steps did you take? What would you do if you faced the situation again?

▼ Think about a time you showed you cared about cash more than others—that you chose to put profit over people. How did it make you feel? How did it make your people feel? What did you or they wish you had done differently? What steps did you take? What would you do if you faced the situation again?

---

advice from different perspectives that they never had. They're talking to me, but I don't know if they're buying any more software from my old company."

The only consolation prize in this story is at least Dave knew where he stood and which side of the Hero Factor his company was on. It never was and never will be a hero and have a culture that valued others. But what happens when a company is a hero and faces that change? That's exactly what happened in our next story.

CHAPTER 12

A **TAXING** SITUATION
WHEN CULTURES
RISE . . . AND FALL

I couldn't possibly recall all the times the Statue of Liberty has waved at me. Sorry, I meant *a* Statue of Liberty, not *the*. I'm not delusional. In fact, chances are you have had this happen to you too, as you drove or walked past one of the 4,000 Liberty Tax stores nationwide. The third-largest retail tax-preparation business in the United States, Liberty Tax employs more than 12,000 people each year to dress up as Statues of Liberty during tax time, a job that dates to the earliest days of the company. In addition to waving at cars and pedestrians, the men and women Liberty employs must smile and be cheerful. Many do more than that and are clearly having a blast even in bad weather when they are not required to be outside, making what they do fun for everyone, which is why I always wave back.

All those Statues of Liberty are not about amusement alone. They are a powerful sales and marketing tool: The vast majority of customers who walk into Liberty Tax do so because of them, and one two-hour shift in the costume nets on average one new customer. Moreover, those smiles also reflected the culture of Liberty Tax—that is, until it decided to go public. It is now working to reclaim its hero culture and Hero Intensity. Liberty learned an important lesson about cultures for all of us—public or private, big or small: **If your company or leadership changes, your people should be right there with you . . . unless you forget to value them.**

WHEN BAD CULTURES HAPPEN TO GOOD COMPANIES

Let's get a few things out of the way before we continue: Change in business does *not* have to change a culture and cost you your people, unless the company and leaders want it to. A change in leadership, a merger, a round of layoffs, an IPO, being acquired . . . all these things are common in business today. Almost every company and leader will go through at least one of them. If you have coached your people well and created a culture that honors them, your people, customers, and partners will follow you into that change, believing in and trusting you, as we heard earlier from Catherine Monson, when she was hired as the CEO of Fastsigns International. Even if the news is bad, they will stand by you, because you have proved your value to them. This goes for Bottom Liners as much as Hero companies and Good Cos. The problem comes when you do one or both of the following: You fail to coach your team to honor those values and they fail to serve you, or your leaders and organization forget about their Hero Intensity in a quest for Operational Excellence and thus fail to serve others. The latter is what happened at Liberty Tax.

Martha O'Gorman, chief marketing officer (CMO) at Liberty, has been with the company since it was founded more than two decades ago. She told me candidly that she believes the decision to go public was "one of the worst things that has happened to Liberty Tax Service in our history." Before that, the company had the belief and trust of its people, and then lost it when the company went public. This was not due to all the things that go along with choosing to become publicly traded and abiding by the complex rules of Sarbanes-Oxley. Those adjustments, similar to when a company is acquired by another, can give any company fits as it struggles to adapt and assimilate its operations to new ways of doing things. This can be even harder when the changes are not a consequence of failure but a consequence of success. It's much harder to adapt when you're doing things right than when you're being bought for pennies on the dollar!

No, "onerous" rules and regulations were one thing to Martha, but the toll the change took on the culture of Liberty was another. To her mind, the company had built a great culture that was transparent, open to listening, organizationally flat, and always caring. But the value of valuing others was lost when Liberty became a publicly traded company, and according to Martha, it turned "into teams of people who didn't trust each other. It made working there not fun anymore. I'd never experienced anything like it in my entire life."

It started small—little things that could be rationalized away as chafing against operational changes. As I said before, many Hero companies find their Hero Intensity challenged by leaders and shareholders who are Bottom Liners and thus prioritize Operational Excellence. Martha freely admits she was annoyed at having to track and document every nickel and dime, something she had never been required to do before. She understood Liberty was hardly ship-shape when it came to things like expenses, but it wasn't slipshod—it *was* a tax company, after all. Yet that's how Martha felt she was treated when she didn't have a receipt for a $6 cab ride. Like she was trying to put one over on them. Like she was careless. Like she was a problem just starting to grow.

Then when she failed to follow a new system for documentation for contract reviews to seize a marketing opportunity she thought was in the best interests of the company, she wasn't asked to defend her actions; she was simply punished. Her credit card limit was chopped from $100,000 a month to $20,000 a month, and shortly afterward her card was declined at a hotel because she was over her limit. Of course, Martha had personal credit cards she could use, but that wasn't the point: "The point is that I thought I was a trusted employee," she says. "I'm responsible for a $20 million advertising budget. Nothing they did said that they trusted me." In other words, it wasn't the rules but how the people enforcing them made her *feel* when they told her, "You better not have lost the receipt because if you did, you are going to have to pay that bill yourself."

I'm not a big fan of zero tolerance and single-mindedness. At the very least, I believe they fail to create a culture of forgiveness and flexibility and make kindness and understanding a whole lot harder. But that does not mean they're *wrong*. They just create a certain kind of culture; in this case, a culture that made Martha and others at Liberty feel like management didn't value them as much as the bottom line or trust them to care about it—because they didn't care about feelings. They just wanted compliance. "Is that really how you keep your employees happy? And especially your high-performing employees?" Martha wonders. More disconcerting was the thought that if management was willing to talk to and treat the CMO this way, what was happening to the people farther down the food chain? What was happening to the franchises, the lifeblood of the company?

And that's where Martha "started to lose it"—and saw Liberty losing it as well.

REMEMBER: CULTURE IS SOMETHING YOU FEEL

Losing the culture that made Liberty fun and a great place to work was like losing the workplace manifestation of those Statues of Liberty. Martha remembered the company's startup days, when it had no money, but people stayed because they believed in the people leading the company and their vision for what it could be. Senior employees took second mortgages and put the money into the company's future. They voluntarily went for months without getting paid, because they believed everything would come out OK. And when they did, the reward for their sacrifice was more stock and raises. This was a company that had seemingly unassailable Hero Intensity until the public offering and leadership change, and then it all started to fall apart in ways that went well beyond expense receipts and credit card limits.

> *Hero cultures are not self-sustaining. Fail to care or be aware of problems as the company faces change, and your Hero Intensity will take a big hit.*

In public documents, according to Martha, and financial disclosures, some of Liberty's executive management team "got huge raises and retention bonuses and were awarded more stock options—while the rest of the people who had been there for years and working their tails off got nothing." Martha, the CMO and one of the original founders of the company, got $8,000, while the people most compliant with the new ownership's demands got much more. Martha declined the money and says she would have if it was $108,000: "I told them, 'I'm sorry. This is an insult. Furthermore, I would like you to take that money and give it to some people who need raises because that is far more important to me than $8,000.' It was wrong. When you have that kind of—and I will say this word because I believe it—when you have that kind of 'evil' at the top, they don't care about the people. In fact, my thought is that they were packaging the company up in order to try to sell it. So they didn't really care as long as they got all their money out of it."

Not everyone felt like Martha. People who were fired or left had severance packages, and Martha saw them "laughing all the way to the bank. They got what they wanted." But on her "side" were the people who got little or nothing. Soon there were more layoffs, and every one hit Martha hard. No one was safe. Everyone was a number. Sure, Martha realizes Liberty's experience isn't unique:

"This happens all the time when a company goes public or a VC or equity partner comes in and buys it," she says. "It can totally change the culture of the company to the point where people are hanging on by their fingernails because they're hoping for better days to come, while others that run for the hills just went and got other jobs." This wasn't the culture that made Liberty Tax a hero company anymore. This wasn't the company Martha knew. Liberty now had what she calls "groups of people working underneath the covers, so to speak, to try to gain power and rip power away from the people who had founded and built the company." With siloed, territorial behavior leading to power plays and hidden agendas caused by the people from the outside—people who didn't have the deep loyalty and belief in the company the leaders on the inside did—Liberty's Hero Intensity tanked.

As Martha says, "I think that when people or companies start to think about the prestige or the notoriety that might go along with becoming publicly traded, they also need to take a look at that and what that really means, and what that could possibly do to the culture and the organization within the company. It was just a travesty what happened and how people were treated, and yet there are folks there that are still coming to work every day and doing the best that they can to try to make a difference. We've been in business for 20 years and never once had a RIF [reduction in force]; never had a layoff. And when this new team got involved and really started to expand their tentacles into the fiber of the company, we had three RIFs in one year. I mean, you're looking at people, many of whom had given 10 or 15 years of their lives, that were unceremoniously let go with very little severance. Not even a little gold statue saying, 'Thank you for your service.'"

Martha soon confirmed her instincts that this would soon affect the bottom line, not just the culture. The change wasn't just affecting corporate headquarters but also Liberty's 4,000 offices nationwide, many of them franchises. The culture of the company extends to them and directly connects to the customers Liberty needs to grow. Unhappy franchisees? Unhappy customers. Unhappy growth numbers.

Martha says she and the people who understood the franchise problem did everything they possibly could to protect them and minimize what they were feeling. But those franchisees and their employees were getting bombarded with questions from their neighbors, ministers, families, and other people they live and work with in their communities.

Liberty couldn't hide what was going on: As a public company, the news was freely available. In fact, everything Martha told me and I wrote here has been documented, disclosed, and filed with the SEC, and much of it has been reported by the media. But having the facts of the story didn't help the franchisees understand what it meant to them. All they knew was Liberty didn't seem to value anyone anymore—or care about what had once been. For example, Liberty's business peaks around tax time. In the past, Liberty had loaned money—say, $30,000, Martha told me—to help some franchises make it to tax season, when that money could be easily repaid. Now the Bottom Liners who were making the funding decisions were bankrupting those franchises by refusing to do so. Zero tolerance.

> *If you don't value others and your Hero Intensity in the workplace, the likelihood is small your partners and customers will trust you to value them—even if you did before.*

As Liberty Tax moved fully into Bottom Liner territory, leaders like Martha, stripped of their power to help operationally as they had in the past, became Struggling Do-Gooders, flailing to retain some balance. "We used to be defined by how we shored people up in times of need. Whether it be business needs or personal needs, the company was always there," Martha says. "Liberty was always ready to step up and help. If somebody's husband died in the middle of tax season, we sent people there to run the business for them because otherwise it would've had to shut down. We lent people money to get into our business because they were passionate about doing it and we saw an opportunity to bring a great person on as a franchisee. Those kinds of things were the things that made us great. Because we cared, and we did things for people that other companies might not have done. And, you know, all that stopped. And the ones that were hurt by it were the ones that needed help and were refused it.

"These things have me struggling every single day to understand how human beings can treat each other so poorly," Martha adds. "It was cruel, and it really took away a lot of my faith in human beings in general."

YOUR PEOPLE HAVE THE POWER

If this or anything like it happened to your business, what would you do? If your mission wasn't to make a Bottom Liner company, how would you restore what was lost? How do you turn something like this around, knowing you have to meet shareholders' expectations for Operational Excellence *and* your people's expectations for Hero Intensity?

1. Begin by taking the advice attributed to the legendary Zig Ziglar that resonates throughout this book and with every entrepreneur and leader (and indeed human): The first step in solving a problem is recognizing that it exists.
2. Next, DO SOMETHING about it. Don't just apologize for it—hold yourself and the entire organization accountable to a strategy for changing it with more than a Band-Aid and vague promises.
3. Finally, restore balance between the two sides—between the Bottom Liners and Struggling Do-Gooders, between profit and people—and raise your Hero Factor again by working toward shared goals. No blame, just recognizing there is a problem and moving forward with a clear eye on what was lost: **people power**.

In the face of its struggles, Liberty had a mirror moment regarding its Hero Factor and followed all these steps. "The most important thing at Liberty is we saw what was happening," Martha says. "It took several months, but as it started to unravel, we saw our franchise base was being significantly scarred by decisions that were being made by some of the newer management. And I will tell you that one thing that we all have in common is our concern about the health of our franchise system and the happiness of our franchisees and how disregarding the happiness of our employees was causing that." Thus, the two sides came to the table and struggled to answer the hard questions together and bring back both their Operational Excellence and Hero Intensity: What should be their next move? How could they make the next tax season excellent to get the company's pride and confidence back? How could they make the franchisees feel the way they used to feel ten years ago?

> *People don't serve companies; they serve people—their leaders. If leadership doesn't value them, why would they believe the company does?*

"A lot of why we stumbled had to do with the fact that we brought in people from outside who didn't necessarily share our passion for the business," Martha says. "But they also didn't share our desire to make sure that our franchisees and our employees were well taken care of and still happy in their jobs. We're not a high-paying company in the scheme of things, but everything that goes along with the culture of being an employee at Liberty Tax Service makes up for the $10,000, $15,000, or $20,000 more that you might be able to make if you went someplace else."

Of course, as we will see in the next chapter, sometimes to move forward, you do need to let some people go. People on the inside of a company can be as much of a culture problem as Bottom Liners brought in from the outside. Many times, people who have been working at a company a long time—perhaps too long—have stopped sharing the values of the company, have become resistant to change, and can cause the same kind of silos and bad moods that developed at Liberty. But just as often, they can be the ones who want and are ready to help the company grow—if you valued others before, they still have that belief and trust. They are ready to serve when asked.

A leader with Martha's experience, credibility, and leadership skills could have left Liberty and gotten a job the next day working anywhere she wanted, from a corporate giant to a startup looking to tap into her ability to grow a company from scratch. But she wouldn't do it because she cared so deeply—and she wasn't alone. That's what makes her ordeal with Liberty different from Dave Sanderson's experience at his software company. Martha *knew* Liberty Tax had been built by people who cared, and she knew she was not the only person left at the company who felt that way: "Our founder, John Hewitt, always said, 'You're going to have to kill me to stop me,'" she says. "Well, I've kind of adopted that as well; my philosophy is, 'You're going to have to kill me to get me out of Liberty before I let it get too sick.' I care that much about it. I'm speaking from my heart, and I think you would hear that from any number of the people who are left that have been here since the beginning, who are fighting with everything they have to stop this from getting any worse. They're staying not only because I stay but also because they care."

So did the person Liberty chose as its CEO to lead the charge to reclaim its Hero Intensity: Nicole Ossenfort, a franchisee who had been with the company for more than a decade. She had seen the passion and the fiber of Liberty Tax Service and borrowed money from her mom so she could be a part of it. Over the next 13 years, she built one of the top franchises in Liberty's system. Martha knew Nicole was the right choice: "She remembered what it felt like to be respected and treated well," she says. "She didn't need to take this job. She has a thriving business and was living a great life in Rapid City, South Dakota. She had built a brand-new house up in the mountains— absolutely gorgeous. Her family is there. But because she believed so deeply in Liberty and the people of Liberty, she uprooted her entire life and moved to Virginia Beach to make sure that we keep ourselves on track."

When you have dedicated people like that, you have a good chance of reclaiming or reinventing your business and your culture. *Because you had one in the first place.* Martha O'Gorman knows this: "I think we're going to be bigger," she says. "I think we're going to be stronger and better than we were before. In fact, we're calling it the rebirth of our software, the rebirth of our culture, and the rebirth of the organization in general. Because it will happen. I'm 100 percent committed to that, and I think that the management is as well. We will be a hero company again. Just a matter of how long it's going to take."

PICK A SIDE!

When an organization and its leadership face real change, even the best will suffer fallout. It can create confusion, especially among your people. Maybe you made a conscious decision to coach them and explain the change, or maybe you decided not to tell them anything, or maybe your strategy fell somewhere in between. Maybe you chose Liberty's path and stopped doing everything: from being stingy with money to everyone but the top of the organization to not caring about how your decisions affect your people, both the ones you were laying off *and* retaining. Soon other employees leave. You lay off more people, good people. Chaos ensues.

But if you do any of those things, you should openly decide to be that company. Nothing is more duplicitous than a Bottom Liner that talks out of both sides of its mouth. Well, except a Zero company that lies about its Operational Excellence and Hero Intensity while lining the pockets of its leader or leaders.

▼ If you're going to be a Bottom Liner, pick a side and be the best Bottom Liner you can be.

▼ If you're going to be a Hero, pick a side, care about and value others, and *do that* to the best of your abilities.

▼ If you're going to be anything else (Good Co., Struggling Do-Gooder) and want to stay there, pick a side and do that.

Until you choose your side, any decisions you make will leave a trail of debris like the tail of a comet flying through your organization, covering your people in confusion.

Liberty Tax made a choice. It decided to move from Hero to Bottom Liner, and that choice cost the company first its Hero Intensity and eventually its Operational Excellence. It discovered that Operational Excellence can be far less resilient than the culture backing it. Because in the end, Liberty's culture problem is a story of resilience. It's a story of mindset. When the company failed at living the values that had made it a Hero company and subsequently lost its Operational Excellence, it had its mirror moment and realized, "*Holy @#$*!*—maybe we need to make a different choice." For them it was not too late. A great company culture can weather assaults like that to the very end. Even if it is barely breathing, it can not only survive but thrive, as long as some people you once valued are still there, or you can bring them or others like them back. Sure, sometimes it's too

---

BE A HERO: ONE MORE CULTURAL MIRROR MOMENT

Thinking about Martha and Liberty Tax's story, look at yourself in the mirror and reflect on a time you found the culture of your business tested by changes big or small to the workplace or marketplace:

▼ What choice did you make and what side did you pick?

▼ How did you handle it?

▼ How did it make you feel?

▼ How did it make your people feel?

▼ What do you or they wish you had done differently?

▼ What would you do differently if you faced the situation again?

---

late to turn the tide. But Liberty chose to restore balance before it drove itself into the ground and believes it can become a Hero again by re-earning the trust of the people inside and outside the company while still delivering results.

When you have faced the same choice, what have you decided? What will you choose next time?

CHAPTER 13

INCLUSIVE CULTURES
HERO OR
STATUS QUO?

Over the past decade, Google spent millions of dollars mining a prodigious amount of data on its workplace and ultimately delivered two detailed reports on what makes great leadership and teams: Project Oxygen (2009, which identified what the best managers at the company do) and Project Aristotle (2016, which identified what makes teams most effective). Both studies commanded attention in *The New York Times* and other media. And what were some of the key findings of the cutting-edge, future-looking, uber-progressive tech company? That people need to listen. That managers need, among other things, to be good coaches, to be interested in team members' success, and to have a clear vision. That teams must have structure, clarity, purpose, and impact. That there is no replacement for having real relationships with your people, especially when it comes to having difficult, important conversations.

If you said, "Duh!" to any or all those things, I don't blame you. They *are* essential to great leadership and building great teams—and thus essential to your Hero Intensity. But they are also pretty basic stuff—there's nothing there we haven't heard before. They may also be a bit ironic coming from Google, which in 2018 revealed its latest effort to remove human interaction from everyday life: Duplex, an AI bot that sounds human, can carry on conversations, and acts as your personal voice assistant.

I also found some irony in Google's reports when it came to a story about the company that broke the year before Duplex was announced. It's a story that strikes at the heart of why the things that make for great leaders and teams are easy to identify but difficult to execute on a consistent and sustained basis—*and* just how hard it is to build truly inclusive cultures.

YOU CAN ASK GOOGLE ANYTHING, BUT WHAT IF YOU QUESTION GOOGLE?

According to *The New York Times* article, one of the key characteristics of great teams identified by Project Aristotle is "psychological safety," meaning a team culture in which people feel safe to take risks, speak up, and have real conversations. Psychological safety is about allowing your people to express their identities without fear of negative consequences to their jobs or careers. Simply put, it's the ultimate expression of *inclusion*; it means listening to what might make you uncomfortable to respect differences, unite around shared goals, and make teams and individuals stronger.

I'm a big fan of psychological safety and have thought about the idea since 2014, when Glenn Llopis of the Glenn Llopis Group, a corporate consulting firm, spoke to my C-Suite Network. His extensive research on thousands of employees showed the number-one thing employees want from their leaders, teams, and organizations—more than respect, recognition, or transparency—was the safety to be themselves and speak "free of judgment." This is not about kumbaya; it's about *booyah!* It's about building inclusive cultures that get *results* from all people and all kinds of people. Each person can own who they are, accept individual differences, and still unite to pursue opportunities and grow the company and themselves.

That's what makes truly inclusive cultures into hero cultures. They don't automatically reject any ideas that do not absolutely conform to their way of thinking. That's exactly what James Damore, a conservative white male engineer at Google, claimed was happening at the company in 2017 just one year after its Project Aristotle report talked about the importance of psychological safety. The claim was part of a widely circulated memo Damore wrote called "Google's Ideological Echo Chamber" that ultimately led to his dismissal and a very public battle between him and Google that played out across traditional and social media, as well as the courts, which ruled that Damore had been legally fired.

Now, before I go any further, know many people told me not to write about this story. Those of you familiar with it might already have your backs up just from the basic facts I laid out, ready to attack. Which is, of course, exactly why I like it. Because the point of this story is to see past those tensions. It doesn't matter whether we agree or disagree or think the actors were right or wrong. The point is that *no one* in this story acts heroically. At its heart, this is a story that shows the complexity of psychological safety and the messiness of inclusion as an absolute rule.

So let's get down to brass tacks: "Google's Ideological Echo Chamber" begins with Damore eviscerating his perceived lack of psychological safety at Google's Mountain View campus when it came to dissent, especially by conservatives like him. He wrote: "Psychological safety is built on mutual respect and acceptance, but unfortunately our culture of shaming and misrepresentation is disrespectful and unaccepting of anyone outside its echo chamber." I have no reason to dispute Damore felt that way in famously liberal

Silicon Valley, and if his memo had gone on to specifically show how he felt he had been shamed and misrepresented Google would have had little legal recourse to fire him. But it didn't.

The memo's opening analysis on psychological safety is somewhat of a red herring for what comes next in the memo—Damore's attack on the company's approach to hiring more female engineers and its goal of achieving a 50–50 gender balance in its workforce. He started off provocatively, asking whether it was a problem to "do arbitrary social engineering of tech just to make it appealing to equal portions of both men and women." He questioned the effect that would have on its current workforce—which was 80 percent male at the time—and argued, among other things, that innate biological and psychological differences made women less suited for the work. Then, using graphs and statistics with footnotes, he attacked what he believed were false assumptions about men and women and their differences. However, some of the figures he cited were misleading, disputed, or extremely limited in scope; some of the evidence Damore cited about the differences between women and men was selective and based on some less-than-solid science. In other words, Damore created his *own* "echo chamber" of an argument. While he concluded with disclaimers, like saying he hoped "it's clear that I'm not saying that diversity is bad," he did himself no favors with his evidence and arguments.

Damore published his memo on Google's internal network, the website Gizmodo soon got ahold of it, and Google fired Damore within a month—not for criticizing the company and pointing out its biases, but for "perpetuating gender stereotypes" that would make for a less inclusive culture for women and added up to what Google considered harassment—because he sent the memo to everyone at the company at the same time by releasing it on the company server, not sharing his views privately with management first. Whether that would have made a difference or not—Damore had no complaints against him by any employee, female or male, before the memo's release—it is not hard to see how it contributed to creating a hostile workplace for some. Moreover, according to Google's legal defense, two women did withdraw their candidacy for positions at Google following Damore's memo, fearing a hostile workplace. The National Labor Relations Board (NLRB) cited these statements in upholding the legality of Google's dismissal of Damore.

> *Inclusive means including all people and thinking;*
> *anything else is exclusive.*

For the record, I don't take issue with Damore's firing or the ruling by the NLRB. Damore's statements were unprotected speech and cost Google talent in addition to his own. I also see Hero Intensity in Google's recognition that it was stuck in its story about its hiring practices and lack of diversity in the workplace, that the lack of women in engineering is an issue, that many Silicon Valley and tech cultures are like frat houses, hostile or even toxic to women, and that something must change to address that in its hiring policies. That said, I also see some truth in the argument that Google's firing of Damore was basically a PR exercise. It's an open question whether that firing will lead to actual change at the company and help it get unstuck from its story since it has shown very little ability to increase any "minority" representation in its workforce despite several well-publicized diversity and inclusion efforts.

Simply put, men are far from a minority in Silicon Valley, and it may be that at this point they have lost any sense of what inclusion, let alone diversity, even means—for women and others. According to a 2017 Bloomberg survey of 1,400 tech employees, "Ninety-four percent of American tech workers give the industry, their companies, and their teams a passing grade on diversity. That's in a sector where 76 percent of technical jobs are held by men, and blacks and Latinos make up only 5 percent of the workforce." Moreover, Google has little to show from past hiring initiatives for attracting minorities to its workforce. Why? I don't know. It's *Google*! They should have people of all shapes, sizes, genders, and colors lined up waiting to work there. But they don't. So was Damore the problem, or was it men in general who created the culture?

This is why it's possible to see Damore as a bit of a sacrificial lamb even if you completely agree with his firing. Google's workplace remains largely male. Does the fact that Damore is gone mean all the men at Google now feel free to fly their feminist flags? Of course not! Misogyny has a long history in American workplaces, and liberal Silicon Valley is no exception. This is also why it's possible to see the legal solution in Damore's case as treating the symptom, not the cause—and failing to achieve truly inclusive psychological safety, which requires some discomfort and a lot of coaching and work to achieve. Damore said he was aware Google was intolerant of "ideas and evidence that does not fit a certain ideology," but he hoped Google would consider what he had to say, "treat people as individuals," and avoid tribalism. Again, Damore did himself no favors with the substance of his memo, but is it so hard to see that Google was *not* sticking to one of its core Project Aristotle values? As a man and part of the majority at Google, Damore might seem to have limited claims to psychological safety (and, again, when you publish a missive for the whole company to see, you are in effect waiving the right to some of that safety). But the partial truth in his story, as noxious as some might find it, is he just wanted his leaders to confront their biases and consider another side: that Google had not been inclusive to his beliefs *and* women.

Whether you defend Damore or Google, demonize them both, or fall somewhere in between, the whole thing makes me uncomfortable—which is the point. Because there are no heroes here. While Google raised its Hero Intensity on one scale (an initiative to hire more women), it lowered its Hero Intensity on another (not finding a way to bring all voices to the proverbial table, especially those that disagree). Google could have fired Damore *and* used the opportunity to turn the spotlight of accountability on itself and asked what it was doing to bring *all* voices into the discussion. Instead, it reaffirmed the status quo and thus lowered its Hero Intensity. Of course, it also must have been thinking, in terms of Operational Excellence, that the long-term gain to its culture and talent outweighed the short-term publicity hit and potential backlash.

Again, I'm not saying that's right or wrong, it's just a choice, and one that shows how messy Hero Intensity can get when it comes to the status quo. No matter how you stack it, the Google story shows just how hard true inclusive leadership is when it comes to appreciating differences and having the courage to welcome all people—even those with whom we have a deep ideological difference: *Choices that reinforce our comfort and demand conformity are always the easiest ones; they silence and exclude the differences that make true Hero cultures.*

In an echo chamber, you don't hear anything but your own voice. In a culture, you can't be what you can't see. Do you see *all* your people? Where are you're own echo chamber?

PICK A SIDE! INCLUSIVE (HERO) OR EXCLUSIVE (STATUS QUO)

Simply put, whether we're talking about gender, race, ethnicity, sexual orientation, political affiliation, religious views, age . . . organizations dealing with these issues and more don't have "diversity problems." They have *inclusion issues.* Valuing others is about choosing to include all people and their differences—both the people who don't look and think like you and those who do. Any choice but the choice to bring *everyone*—*all* people and their different perspectives—to the table and allow them to impact decisions, directions, and growth is exclusive.

That's why Hero cultures:

▼ Welcome anyone who wants to ride with them
▼ Recognize that differences and different ways of doing things do not mean that the people with those differences can't, won't, and don't share the values of the organization
▼ Understand non-negotiables are essential when it comes to values, but they are the enemy when they fail to evolve and exclude others simply because they are different or when Operational Excellence is not all that matters

Does that mean you *have* to be inclusive to be a Hero? Of course not. Organizations that have cultures that exclude others can be Heroes to those they choose to include—though doing so may have long-lasting consequences in the court of public opinion. But that's what they are: choices to value conformity, uniformity, and/or familiarity. By looking at them in purely business terms, we can pass over the question of whether we think these choices are right or wrong and look at them simply as *choices*.

Take an example from the business of sports that divided players and fans: the NFL requiring players to stand during the national anthem. The NFL owners have *every* right to demand their players stand during the national anthem as a condition of employment. The players are employees of the league, and the NFL is a big business. The owners believe they are acting in the best interest of the brand and themselves, and the players are not, so they restrict their expression and deny them influence. Instead of finding a way to include the players' voices of protest, the league made an *exclusive* choice, believing those displays hurt the brand among its core customers—who, according to Magna Global's 2017 "U.S. Sports Report," skew older (the average NFL viewer is 50). It is worth noting, however, that another big sports business, the NBA, has taken a different approach. Its owners have required players to stand for the national anthem since the 1980s, but the players have not publicly objected to the policy. Why? Because the NBA has found a way to allow its players to express their opinions before and after games (for example, wearing "I Can't Breathe" shirts during warmup practice) and have more influence on how the league is run. While the NBA has a more diverse fan base and a different (and smaller) organizational structure than the NFL, it nonetheless has made an inclusive choice, finding a way to bridge the gap between what the employees want to say and not alienating its fans.

Few of you will face choices like these in your business, ones that play out in the media and become politically charged topics. But your choices still have consequences, not only to your Hero Intensity but also your Operational Excellence, as everyone you exclude becomes a potential competitor and/or a lost connection to customers.

To be clear, both exclusion *and* inclusion have consequences. Being more inclusive of anything or anyone different is disruptive. New people, new systems, new compliance requirements, new laws—all changes on a certain scale are often not just uncomfortable and difficult but also unsettling and messy (e.g., Apple getting rid of the antiquated standard headphone jack when it introduced the iPhone 7 to make it waterproof, forcing millions of customers to buy a clunky adaptor for their legacy headphones or get new headphones that connect through Bluetooth). Inclusion can alienate those who like the way things were, even if the change is an improvement. And like disruptive businesses that enter a market, inclusion can put companies and people out of business or out of work and force some compromise—or, rather, a more evolved sense of values. But generally, the choice to include leads to those people or organizations that want to preserve the status quo choosing to exclude themselves, refusing to give up anything to gain more.

> *A truly inclusive organization chooses to welcome and invest in difference and serves all people to generate results and performance.*

Inclusive leadership doesn't just raise your Hero Intensity; it should lead to Operational Excellence as well. For example, before she became The Hero Club's general manager, Tricia Benn built a market research team at Rogers Communications, a multibillion-dollar Canadian company, that had both demographic diversity and diversity of thought. When the team was tested during the Great Recession, Tricia says, "our diversity as a team was what gave us strength to innovate and adapt through the worst financial crisis any of us had seen."

Tricia lead the team's charge to change a traditional cost center (market research) into a multimillion-dollar revenue stream. However, it was the strength of the team and its culture of embracing their diversity, innovating with confidence, and solving problems that brought scale to the business. In fact, it became the cornerstone of its resiliency when the economy collapsed and the major brands the company worked with needed strategic, solutions-oriented thinking and problem solving. Tricia's team was able to adapt to help those clients adjust their communications with their customers and partners. The team ended up being the only group in the division to meet its financial targets for the year. "The social and financial benefits of creating a team that celebrates what makes each contribution unique and invaluable to a successful team are extraordinary," Tricia adds. "This team had each other's backs as it built new approaches and solutions that bucked the status quo. It turned a traditional approach to seniority on its head by making each team member serve as a leader and supporter; the more senior your role on the team, the more of a supporter you should be to help your people and company achieve greatness and grow and evolve with what's happening internally and externally."

That's not to say that the status quo is easy to undo—or even that it's possible in the short term. Our legislative and executive branches of the federal government would have you believe that all change must be about a scarcity mentality (win-lose) and not an abundance mentality (win-win). But that's not true, and it is why the Hero way forward will be led by America's businesses, not its politicians. I was particularly struck by a line in *Incredibles 2* when the government forced its heroes into hiding again: "Politicians don't understand people who do good just because it's right."

▼ ▼ ▼

Let's go back to the situation that led to Damore's infamous memo: a lack of female engineers at Google. Actually, there is a lack of female anything at Google and other tech companies. According to a 2018 Statista report, only 20 percent of Google's tech workforce and 31 percent of its overall workforce was female. By comparison, Microsoft had 19 and 26 percent, respectively, and Netflix had 28 and 43 percent. But it's not like there are tons of women just waiting around to be hired: Women receive *less than 20 percent of all engineering degrees* in the United States. That's a problem that can't be fixed with a more inclusive culture and a hiring initiative. Those changes could help retain the women Google has and attract a few more, but it won't bring their numbers up to 50 percent.

The long-term solution would involve a fundamental shift in mindset on how to create a new pipeline of female engineers through retraining the existing workforce and encouraging girls to think about it as a career in high school or even earlier. Those kinds of solutions require new ways of thinking and take years to realize any gains, and the tech world is not known for its patience. They also require genuine effort to create cultures welcoming to women once they get there, which is not something the male-dominated tech world does very well. The National Venture Capital Association reports that in 2017, 89 percent of partners at venture firms were male. That same year, PitchBook Data Inc. recorded $85 billion invested by venture capitalists; $66.9 billion (79 percent) went to startups founded entirely by men and $1.9 billion (2.2 percent) went to startups founded entirely by women. When they could land a deal, women got on average $7 million less.

Again, that's neither right nor wrong but a choice these venture capitalists made, informed, as I said before, by centuries of misogyny in America and decades of misogyny in Silicon Valley, where it is perhaps worse than in any other industry. In other words, the choice isn't random: It's based in a deeply ingrained status quo. It's also not necessarily a loser. I'm sure many of them made money on their male brethren. But do you really think those women and others disenchanted with the lack of opportunity and inclusivity are just walking away? Perhaps some do, but others, like Katrina Lake, stick around and fight. When Lake raised a relatively small amount of venture capital from the men she pitched Stitch Fix to, she simply did less with more. The company, an online personal stylist that mails boxes of clothing to its customers, took off and as of 2018 was valued at nearly $2 billion.

How many more Lakes are out there? How many will be able to bypass the exclusive male cultures that make women like her fight for every dollar and find solidarity with other like-minded people who are ready to help? Many, if women have anything to say about it.

For example, in 2017, a group of more than 30 women in the venture capital industry launched All Raise, a nonprofit organization dedicated to doubling "the number of female partners and increase the percentage of funding going to female founders in the next few years." Female Founder Office Hours is another of its initiatives, which aims to provide increased capital to female founders, give one-on-one advice, and offer mentoring. Julia Hartz, CEO and cofounder of the ticketing company Eventbrite, is one of the more than 100 leaders who have signed up to coach and mentor the next generation of women entrepreneurs and leaders.

That's what the Hero Factor is all about: the future we want for our children. *All* our children. The vision of the Hero is a selfless one that brings people together, working hard to include and welcome all views—even those we disagree with. It can be hard and takes time to do the Hero thing. It can even lead to a drop in Operational

---

BE A HERO: THIS IS THE CULTURE YOU HAVE

Glance around your office and take a hard look at your people. Is it more Hero or status quo: echo chamber or truly inclusive? Here are a few questions to help you out as you think about that and what's next:

▼ Where did you recruit those people? Do they all come from the same place?

▼ How many look, act, and believe exactly as you do beyond the values of the company?

▼ Do you know anything about their identity? How they think?

▼ Are you welcoming of that thinking and do they welcome it in each other?

Excellence if people resist. But I believe that good eventually trumps evil, don't you?

PICK A SIDE! THE FUTURE OR THE PAST

All Raise won't be the last group of its kind—in any industry. The status quo may be deeply entrenched in industries across the country, but it is not invincible. All people—not just women, not just minorities, but all those who have been excluded or are fed up with the lack of inclusivity—will rise up against it.

Consider the finance industry. I once had John LeFevre, author of *Straight to Hell: True Tales of Deviance, Debauchery, and Billion-Dollar Deals* (2015) and the man behind the wildly popular and often amusing Twitter handle @GSElevator (things overheard in the Goldman Sachs elevator), on my radio show. He talked about one post in which women who worked at Goldman and in investment banking in general were used as "tethered goats"—in other words, as eye candy for clients. I admit I wanted to punch him in the throat. He had a daughter (not that that should be the only reason to abhor this practice)! Yet he was telling me that's just the way it is.

No, you're accepting it and saying you condone it because that's the status quo. That's your choice, and it will eventually bite all the hopeless asshats (aka Zeroes) and Wannabes in the ass. Go ahead and preach the status quo and wrap yourself in a warm fuzzy blanket of denial while the rest of us evolve.

Do you know what demographic group by far had the largest growth in terms of the number of businesses founded in the U.S. from 2008 to 2017? Black women, ages 34 to 45. How often did organizations even want to hire these women, let alone do the work to find them? Now they're starting businesses that are going to take away those organizations' customers and potentially their people. In today's business world, if the kings don't make you feel welcome in their castles, you can just build your own. Maybe you can even create a kingdom.

That doesn't just go for women. It goes for anyone who might be called "other" when it comes to your organization's culture and your leadership. *This includes your customers!* In the age of social media, companies have learned they can't ignore customers' demands for change or individual needs, fail to tailor for different demographic groups, not customize, or cut corners without getting found out fast. But many still do anything they can to avoid actually talking to them. I'm not talking about the asshats who exploit their customers for their personal gain. Many do this under the guise of Operational Excellence—underfunding and outsourcing customer service to India or other lower-cost places. That's because they don't value *anyone*.

Listen, even inclusive organizations and leaders are not free of bias—no one is. Say the companies and leaders who rise up against the status quo decide to change their culture by no longer hiring people who reflect that status quo. That's just substituting a new kind of exclusivity. It isn't wrong, but it doesn't raise your Hero Intensity unless the companies' leaders find a way to value all people—even the ones who excluded them in the past. If not as employees, then as partners in some way.

In addition, while I believe all companies should be reflective of their communities and customers to the best of their ability, not all companies that look like the status quo are necessarily exclusive. My office in Sioux Falls doesn't have any black employees, but there are few black people living in South Dakota, so the potential hiring pool is small. They make up less than 2 percent of the state's population, compared to more than 12 percent nationwide, and many of them are employed on or with the Air Force base near Rapid City. The question isn't whether I have any black employees, but rather what would I do if I needed to understand that market better? What if it became an issue for me and my people? What would I do if I found our culture stuck in its story of inclusivity?

How would I start? I'd pick a side! Here's how you do that:

▼ Pick a side! Change it or not.
▼ If the choice is to change, dismiss tribal thinking, make declarative statements, and back them up with tangible steps and action, no matter how uncomfortable it makes you. Be a Hero and welcome all people.

▼ If the choice is not to change, well, that fuzzy blanket of denial must be really comfortable. At least be a Hero to those you value already.

Anyone who thinks even the mightiest, most staid cultures can't do this and still maintain their core values need only look at the 2018 royal wedding between Prince Harry and American actress Meghan Markle. Talk about the most traditional pomp and circumstance: gilded horse-drawn carriages! Stately churches! Women in ridiculous hats! Markle didn't come from that world. The media noted that she was no Diana or Kate. She had no royal or blue blood. She came from across the pond, an actress and daughter of a black mother and a white father and who worked for what she had. Yet she brought her influence to bear on her and Harry's wedding: A black cello player! A gospel choir! Oprah! Yet did anyone from the queen to those of us watching around the world think of it as anything less than a royal wedding—the equal of any that came before?

Harry found Meghan, and England rejoiced in his and its monarchy's choice to be more inclusive. Whatever you choose, please hold yourself accountable to that choice. I may be a huge fan of inclusive cultures and psychological safety, but I have no tolerance for leaders who fail to hold themselves accountable for making the opposite choice when it comes to including people—and deciding who they might need to get rid of.

CHAPTER 14

THE IMPORTANCE OF DECISIVENESS AND LETTING PEOPLE GO

By now, you have seen me use the phrase "pick a side" more than a few times. That's because I mean it. This is a time to choose. This is a defining time for our nation. The best part of our polarized political climate is that more people are involved and speaking up than ever before. On almost every issue on both sides, our best and worst values are being laid bare. I cannot recall another moment in my lifetime when I've seen so many people who normally would politely decline to say something say, "No. This is not me. It doesn't stand for me." And by the way, that's not easy. It takes courage to stand up for what you believe, especially when your side is demanding your fidelity. When ideas and actions are this polarizing, you can lose not only business but also friends if you wind up on the "wrong side."

Personally, even if I hate some of the decisions being made, I love what is going on right now. I love that our best and worst sides are coming to the surface and forcing us to consider what we truly value and how we choose to act. The real questions are, "What's next? What will we choose to do?"

▼ Will our single-mindedness on an issue lead us to choose only those businesses that support our beliefs on that issue but offend us in every other way?

▼ Could we choose to patronize those who do not support the issue we care most about but share our other values?

▼ Or can we do something even greater: turn the spotlight of accountability on ourselves and consider what the words we use to describe our values mean when it comes to valuing others?

For example, consider a word like "integrity"—a value I and many other leaders believe is non-negotiable. Stop to consider what having integrity means. Is it doubling down on the honest moral stances that define the past and your status quo without compromise? Or is it evolving the definition to create a more inclusive culture and be the best you can be for others, right down to the smallest details, regardless of their stance on certain issues?

There is no magic pill for this decision, which is why Hero leaders need to be mindful and thoughtful, listening attentively, and in the end be decisive yet grounded in their leadership. **Simply put, Hero leaders are decision-makers with win-win or abundance mentalities. They are grounded in a vision for what they and their**

> *An inclusive culture needs decisive yet grounded leaders to guide it through uncertainty and change.*

organizations want to achieve and have confidence through the chaos and uncertainty of business today.

A hero culture allows for all kinds of things except drama. When something starts to become a distraction to the core goal you're trying to achieve, then the next quality you see in hero cultures is that they're decisive. They're steering to the north star, they're following a path. Sometimes the path will change, but overall wherever they're going is better than the place they've been.

Maybe I should have said "irrational yet grounded." As I said in my previous book, *Think Big, Act Bigger*, a little irrational leadership is needed to innovate and to drive people together beyond the edge of the table without falling off. It's not good enough anymore to say we're going to go from point A to point B. You need to push beyond to point C, so your people can test the limits of point B and discover what's next. Hero leaders need the energy to talk a little louder, push a little further, and ask what's next without bouncing off the walls. But because they stay grounded, when the team is done pushing and finds the strategies and tactics that will work, the leaders pull them back, decide what the priorities are, and say, "Let's go," empowering the team to execute.

In these moments, leaders will see who on their teams is truly ready to break free from the comfort of the status quo and what their people can do. That's why before the team gathers at that table, leaders must apply their decisiveness and choose to do these two things so their company's culture doesn't get stuck in the story of what it once was:

▼ Reconsider their people.
▼ Rethink how they think about people in their cultures—what they contribute and what they are capable of.

RECONSIDERING YOUR PEOPLE: LET 'EM GO TO COMBAT THE STATUS QUO

Most people and companies don't start off wanting to be asshats. No one wakes up in the morning and says, "I can't wait to be stupid." No one walks into their office and says, "You know, today I'm going to screw everybody. I'm going to rape and pillage and go through people like they're disposable. I'm going to lie and cheat everyone and take as much money as I can for me." The fall usually comes from temptation, desperation, or hubris, and usually over time. Even Bernie Madoff was in business for almost two decades before his Ponzi scheme took shape. Then he shed his Operational Excellence and Hero Intensity and changed his business model to one that served no one but him.

OK, that's a low-lying fruit example of a person and his company failing to value others. But there are smaller stories that go viral every day that should force companies to reconsider their cultures and whether they value all people, especially their customers. The Starbucks manager who called the cops on those two black men in Philadelphia from Chapter 7. United Airlines dragging a passenger off an overbooked flight for refusing to give up his seat. Comcast changing a customer's name on a bill from Ricardo Brown to Ass**** Brown when he canceled his cable subscription. I could go on and on and on. . . . While these customer fails may have been perpetrated by some bad apples, the expression holds true: That apple does not fall far from the tree—or in this case, the culture.

To paraphrase what I said in telling Dave Sanderson's story in Chapter 11: A company that allows those bad apples usually has more, even in seemingly inclusive cultures. Then it turns out those companies really had a culture of "don't ask, don't tell"—and if they do tell, cover your asses and cover it up before it costs the bottom line! Many of the worst actors that organizations protect should have been fired long before movements like #MeToo created a frenzy of firings and a zero tolerance policy for bad acts. In fact, some of the less egregious offenses might have been prevented or corrected without letting someone go if the organization valued the people being wronged more than the company's reputation and bottom line. As I said earlier, what bugs me about all the apologies from organizations that condoned sexual harassment, casually sold our data, failed to acknowledge biased behavior, or ignored the horrible abuse of children (there's a special place in hell for them) is not just how little they valued people over covering their own asses. *It's the fact that the mea culpas turn into mea nothing when it comes to truly changing the culture.*

Even if it's true that there was just one bad apple spoiling that bunch (sorry, last apple analogy), the line from *Pretty Woman* rings true: "The bad stuff is easier to believe." As Bill Wallace, a Hero Club member and founder of Success North Dallas, reminded me, "Keep in the back of your mind that the culture is defined by the worst possible behavior you as a CEO will allow from any one employee or member. Take immediate action to correct the situation or to remove the situation. A lot of times, we fight so hard to make ourselves right in our hearts, make ourselves right in what we've done, that we by doing that jeopardize the rest of the team. So you've got to move forward and remove those that don't fit."

Exactly, which brings up a couple of important points when it comes to letting people go:

▼ There are people you must let go because of bad actions.
▼ There are people you must let go because they don't fit with the culture anymore.

I have deep respect for leaders and organizations that take immediate action to let an employee go when they have a problem that can't be coached out or corrected. I hold even deeper respect for leaders who let people go because the fit just isn't right. Unable to coach people up or out, they make the hard decision to let the person go. Often, that decision turns out to be best for both the team culture and the people being let go. For example, I once had to let go a manager at a franchise I owned. He was only a few years younger than I was at the time, and no matter what I tried, it just wasn't working out. At first, he was really ticked off about it. But I told him honestly, "Look, this isn't the right fit for you, and you're going to be miserable. I know you don't see it now, but it's going to be the right thing." Fast-forward a few years, and a friend told me he ran into the guy. *Oh, and?* "He says that you were one of the best people he ever worked for. And that experience was one of the best experiences in his life and helped him go to the next level."

That said, sometimes letting someone go is not an option. Some organizations have government or union rules that don't allow you to terminate employees easily or at all. The same is true in the world of franchises. While I had the power to fire that manager, franchisees are not employees, and if they're not doing things the right way, you can't just get rid of them. So what do you do? The same thing in both situations: You hold them to standards of excellence and build inclusivity around that.

I like the way Jim Bennett, president and founder of the CFO and financial consulting services firm Now CFO, talks about holding people to the highest standards: "It's been interesting over the years as my business has grown; a lot of folks have come and gone," he says. "It's interesting now: They either fit within our culture or they don't. And the ones that fit have a very high bar of what they're going to do and accomplish, and if they don't have that high bar, they don't like hanging around us. My personal goal is to help people realize the potential that we see in them. Find a little more of themselves. If a person can go home at night and realize that they achieved more than they believed in themselves, it's really fantastic to see how much better they feel about themselves, and yet you get to see them grow, too. That's a culture of moving forward."

Now consider what Catherine Monson, CEO of Fastsigns International, told me about motivating franchisees: "I would say that the most important thing a franchise, and the most important thing any leader, can do is create a great culture that's focused on operation, constant improvement, and integrity. And that works whether it's a company-owned location, a corporate company, or a franchise owner. A lot of that is the same."

Exactly! The key is excellence in moving forward. That's why I hold the utmost respect for those leaders who let go longtime employees who have not been doing anything morally, ethically, or legally wrong but have simply been coasting, getting decent results, but not having to do half the things required of new hires. People they might even like or be friends with. People who haven't evolved with you no matter how much you tried. Lone wolves who couldn't

---

BE A HERO: THE RIGHT FIT

As you did in the last chapter, look around your office, take a hard look at your people, and ask:

▼ Does each person fit the culture of the company?

▼ Does each person serve the values and goals of the company?

▼ Has each person evolved as your company and its values have evolved?

▼ What are the differences between the people who have been with you the longest and the shortest amount of time? Do you expect the same things of them?

▼ How many are stuck in their own story?

---

care less about being more inclusive, doing things differently, collaborating, or sharing with anyone else. These people affect the feel of the culture for others, and the solution is the same for them as for any other employee: If you change a culture, you have an obligation to coach your people to be ready for and through that change. Coach them up, coach them into a new position, or coach them out. You can't be inclusive while excluding some people based on who they are or what they believe. You can get rid of *a person*—an individual—if the fit isn't right, if the steps you've taken to try to make it work are documented.

RECONSIDERING HOW YOU THINK ABOUT YOUR PEOPLE

Whenever a company needs to make a change in personnel, the question must always be: What's next? I hear a lot of lip service to concepts like sacrifice, service, and stewardship when it comes to firing and hiring people and how it will lead to changing cultures, but what's next? What will you do to sustain the culture you want to change or create? Will your company do more than throw money at the problem and create another employee resource group? Will Starbucks follow through on its promise to do more anti-bias training? What good is a new diversity initiative and a donation to the cause of the offended party's choice if you have to keep doing it again and again? Unless that's all you intended to do in the first place!

What are you doing to change your thinking, not just your people, and thus change the culture to make it more inclusive and value all individuals in the long term?

> *Hero companies need to think about and do things differently, do more, and do it again and again and again to change a culture stuck in the status quo.*

To start, you need to change how you think about your people—*and you have to value thinking itself and listen to what others have to say.* So I am going to take my own advice. I've met some really smart people in my life, some of whom have thought very deeply on this topic. Rather than reading more about what I think, here is how a few of them decided to "rethink thinking" when it comes to building inclusive cultures and raising your Hero Intensity.

Stabilizers Get Your Culture Stuck in Its Story

Dr. Rachel MK Headley and Meg Manke, senior partners at The Rose Group International, work with leaders and companies on creating great teams and cultures. They know from experience that understanding how your people work in team environments is going to help you be strategic, roll out changes, improve performance, and increase revenue and results. Implementing such changes can help each organization define its unique culture. The question is: Even if the organization's people love the new direction, will they actually go there?

The answer is usually no—or at least not without guidance. Headley knows that from her previous work. A PhD scientist who spent many years running a government program, she started working with a team on which everyone cared mostly about how much credit they were getting and maintaining the status quo ("exhausting," she says). She then went to a high-performing operational team. She got curious about why those teams were so different, and when she figured it out her goal became to help companies create exceptional internal experience and help them in "a genuine way be more egalitarian." For her and Manke, that has a direct link to valuing others—specifically, valuing the types of people you have. They see people on a team as one of four Culture Types: Independents, Stabilizers, Fixers, and Organizers. None of these types are negative. All of them have plusses and minuses you need to understand to lead them through big cultural transitions. To understand this as it relates to your Hero Factor, they gave me permission to share their graphic explaining the goals and fears of each type (see Figure 14.1, on page 166), created from their considerable experience and research and explained in detail in their book, *iX Leadership: Create High-Five Cultures and Guide Transformation*.

Transitions can feel chaotic for all these types. For Fixers and Independents, this is no big deal—they enjoy (even revel in) the unexpected that comes with change. Stabilizers and Organizers don't. If Organizers can create order in the chaos and understand it, they can deal with it just fine. They don't like it, but they sort it out. But stabilizers generally hate change. That's why they are particularly attracted to steady, predictable jobs, like those in manufacturing or at NASA where there's one way to do a job "right." According to Headley and Manke's research, it can take Stabilizers *years* to get through a significant change to an organization and its culture; some never do, like the guy that gets asked to get put back "on the floor" after he's been promoted to a management job and doesn't like it. That doesn't mean Stabilizers are "bad," mind you. In fact, Headley and Manke call them "the glue that holds the culture together." Stabilizers just like

Figure 14.1 Culture Types from The Rose Group International

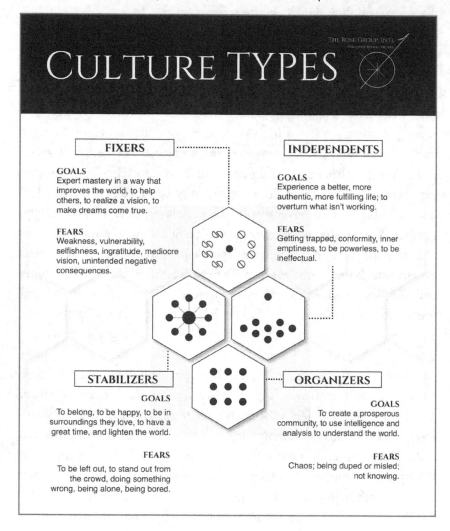

predictability every single day, boots on the ground, and getting stuff done. They won't leave you or the team, unless things get really bad for a really long time.

Which is also the problem: Headley and Manke have found the average percentage of Culture Types in the general population are 17 percent Organizers, 18 percent Independents, 22 percent Fixers, and 43 percent Stabilizers. Combine that Stabilizer number with the Organizers, and you have 60 percent of your team that dislikes change lined up against the 18 percent of Independents who are self-driven and love chaos and flexibility. They just want to innovate—to be free to find the best opportunities and possibilities. But they freak out when you put too many restrictions on them. They need freedom—like me! But if 60 percent of your people are the opposite of that, what often happens? Your team culture can and will get stuck in its story. It will resist and prevent change no matter how hard the Independents push.

So how do you get those three types to work together? Fixers! Behind every successful independent CEO, there is at least one Fixer helping translate the chaotic energy into something that everyone else can get behind. Fixers strive for inclusiveness. They see all sides, differences, and strengths in each type. They make them work together with the shared goal of results and a winning team—like Manke and Headley! If Fixers can't move the Stabilizers along, they look to bring more Fixers, Independents, and Organizers in. Because as Headley and Manke have found, if just 30 percent of your team buys into the new vision, you can move the culture and the company in a new direction. So, get everyone together and let them figure out how to move their story forward—or change it!

Bring Your Best Thinking Together

In Chapter 6, I discussed how Topgolf Entertainment Group executive chairman Erik Anderson channels the human need to be creative and create experiences for its guests and fans. This requires what he calls a culture of "intellectual integrity" that allows the business to evolve beyond best practices to best thinking. To get this best thinking at Topgolf, Anderson does not use the word *inclusive*. He draws on a math term: fractals.

Fractals are beautiful geometric figures in which each part has the same character as the whole. At Topgolf, this means each person is "not competing with each other but working collaboratively together on this form"—a form each person is thinking about equally. But, Anderson explains, for this to genuinely work, a culture must have that psychological safety: "People realize they have a safe place to operate," he says. "It's fun. It's creative. And they can bring their own creative ideas along the way. This model has a lot of integrity to it. It asks, 'What's our best thinking? Where are we going forward? What can we explore? Where can we be curious?' When you create a safe environment, you get curiosity, because curiosity thrives in the safe place. Safe is not comfortable, safe means, 'I can think.' Remember: We said safety is first. I can take the risks, knowing that I'm trying to be curious. I'm exploring. I'm learning. I'm growing. I'm building."

According to Anderson, this "building culture is entirely different than a winning culture," which makes it closer to the Hero Factor balance between Operational Excellence and Hero Intensity. "I spend a lot of time with CEOs right now, and they want to win," Anderson adds. "But what does winning mean? Of course we're going to try to win a particular bid if we're going up against one of our competitors. That's important and great to win. Of course we're going to be competitive. That goes without saying. But we'll be much more successful if, in the long run, we keep building and we have the best products and the best ideas and the best cultures. Building is much more valuable than competing. If we build, we create value. We'll figure out how to share. We'll negotiate."

For those of you who think it's harder to change to this kind of culture at an established company, Catherine Jackson has found it harder than she thought to deploy something similar at her travel startup, My Fave Places. As a former senior vice president at the global financial company Macquarie Group, she often longed for a chance to be curious and work around other curious people. So she demanded it at her new venture, which was not easy: "I now insist on people having curious minds if they're coming to work for me," she says. "I have some really great technical people who have these curious minds, and I've got some great advisors who have that as well. But I learned along the way that people who wanted to join my startup because they think it's really great and fun are not necessarily more curious than the finance people I used to work with. When they actually get down to, 'All right, you've got to investigate something else' and become almost a jack of all trades, too many people suddenly go, 'Oh, I only specialize in this.' I understand if they are coming from a particularly specialized field such as law and that is their only training, but they should still go out and find out more or ask more questions. Don't say, 'I'm sorry. I couldn't do it' or 'I can't do it.' I need people who think differently to talk to one another and then are able to go and seek information on their own and actually do the discovery process of 'doing.'"

I not only like that but also think there is one part of almost every organization that could do more to make the entire culture better—if organizations would let it happen.

Make Human Resources about Human Capital

Almost every company of a certain size has a human resources person or department, and they are usually the ones working on the diversity and inclusion initiatives designed to bring new and different talent to an organization. Ironically, then, if there is any department that is routinely *excluded* from discussions about the growth of the business at most companies, it is HR. Yet HR people are the only ones who connect to every department and person inside an organization and are often the gateway for new talent. They could deliver measurable value if organizations and leaders allowed them to do what Erik Anderson said: build. Build organizational capabilities, strengthen systems, and, most important, empower human capital.

So why do so many leaders and organizations see HR as simply compliance people? The ones meeting hiring quotas and enforcing rules and codes of conduct? Because usually that's all they are allowed to do, when they could do so much more. On my show, I spoke to Dave Ulrich, a University of Michigan professor known as the "father of modern HR," about his book *Victory Through Organization: Why the War for Talent Is Failing Your Company and What You Can Do About It* (McGraw-Hill Education, 2017). He sees HR professionals as I do: perfectly positioned to respond to emerging opportunities and deliver much more value.

Because their job is to value everyone at an organization.

As Ulrich told me, the HR profession today is evolving from an internal focus on people to an external focus on the organization, and how well it can serve its customers to create value. HR executives can develop the right competencies to evolve with the demands of this new trend. They can prove what they do will impact business value and competitiveness. He and his co-authors have the data to prove it: 30,000 survey respondents from 1,400 companies. The findings demonstrate that organizational success isn't just about the talent a company has, it's also about how the collective organization makes the individual talent better. HR people are perfectly positioned to do all that and help leaders know what they don't know inside and outside a company. They can break down walls to the outside and silos on the inside. They can also help find external partners who match the values of the company.

For example, I heard a story about a hospital in Boston that wanted to increase its number of minority nurses to better reflect the populations it serves. That statement in and of itself does *not* make you a hero unless it is backed by tangible steps to bring those people in *and* make the culture more inclusive to retain them. What you need is someone internally who understands the company culture, who not only can represent that culture to the candidates but also represent the company to partners who can find the talent your company needs. That's HR.

HR could include all kinds of human capital—the capital you want and need *and* the capital you already have. They could be the bridge to partners and joint ventures with other organizations that must work with each other, because none of them have the knowledge and human capital to do it on their own. United, they could add value to everyone, including the customers.

In the end, what these three examples have in common is they strive to create inclusive cultures built on a foundation that allows people to be entrepreneurial. Allowing your people to exist as individuals—who come together as a team to serve you as their leader and the goals of the company—boosts both your Hero Intensity and your Operational Excellence. But maintaining those Hero Factor heights requires more, because none of what we just discussed sustains itself without continuously valuing the human capital you already have.

If I were that hospital trying to hire more diverse talent? The first thing I would do isn't hire a consultant, send out a press release, or even reach out to a potential partner. I'd do what HR could do: understand the talent I already have, talk to them, and listen to what they had to say. That's one of the key things every leader needs to do to sustain a hero culture and attract more people to it.

CHAPTER 15

HERO
RELATIONSHIPS
LISTENING, VULNERABILITY, TRUST, AND ALIGNMENT

In the 50-plus years since it aired the last of its 249 episodes, *The Andy Griffith Show* has always been available, either in syndication or streaming. People from all generations have discovered and loved it, perhaps for its strong moral center and the civility at its core. Perhaps as an escape to its more (literal and figurative) black-and-white values—a version of the status quo some people want to return to. Perhaps because the show, especially Don Knotts as Deputy Barney Fife, is *still* funny. *The Andy Griffith Show* has always been with me—its first episode debuted just before I did—and I remember watching the show growing up. Today, as an adult, I still watch when I come across it and even use something I learned from an episode in my business today.

THE BLACKBALL

In the 1966 episode "The Lodge," Andy talks to Howard Sprague about becoming a member of the Mayberry men's Lodge Club. Howard is interested, and Andy invites him to the next meeting to check it out. He has a good time and tells Andy he wants to join. He understands that unless he gets a "blackball" from a current member, he's in. As it turns out, Howard's mother is none too thrilled about her son joining the club, so she lies and tells Goober that Howard's father is addicted to playing cards and Howard might become addicted, too. Goober's blackball is the only one Howard gets. When Howard visits the club one more time and Goober frantically tries to hide all the cards, the lie is revealed. Understanding prevails, Goober removes his blackball, and Howard is welcomed as a member. (Thank the Lord Howard did not have Facebook or Twitter to rail against Goober and the club or the solution might not have been so neat.)

Interestingly, the lie becomes truth: Howard becomes addicted to cards. Even in Mayberry, life is not as black and white as it seems. And neither is inclusion when it comes to hero cultures and valuing others, which is why my team and I have a blackball of our own.

> *What happens when something feels off?*
> *Do you have a way for your people to express*
> *themselves and feel they have influence?*

The word *blackball* has a pretty dark legacy in America, so let me get two things out of the way before I continue. First, the blackball we use in my business is about open and honest communication, not false beliefs, hidden agendas, and lies like the one Howard's mom told. Second, I believe everyone has the right to speak, believe, and live as they choose, as long as it does not deny the rights of or hurt others. The blackball has nothing to do with blanket exclusions and bias. It can't be used against anyone on the basis of race, ethnicity, gender, religion, country of origin, accent, sexual orientation, criminal history, physical disability, age, weight, how they dress . . . That's illegal in most cases and wrong for so many more.

Wrong because, as we just covered, hero companies and leaders know they always need to work hard to make sure they are recruiting and reaching the best talent to create inclusive environments that respect all individuals, honor differences, and unite around goals. This often involves some discomfort as values and cultures evolve. But inclusiveness doesn't mean everyone fits or should fit or will fit every culture, hero or not. Culture, especially mood and morale, is about feel, and people determine that feel. We discussed dealing with fit for the people you have in the last chapter. The blackball is about the people you let in.

Now, most of the time decisions about who to hire or welcome to our organization have no need for blackballs. There is a clear preference for one candidate over the other. While everyone might not get their top choice, they can, should, and will stand behind the choice a team or company makes. But what if a team member just feels "off" about someone? The blackball allows a team member to share those feelings—and have the power to influence decisions, even if it goes against the rest of the team.

In a genuinely inclusive culture, the blackball does not exclude lightly. It forces people to think about the consequences of their actions, see all sides, confront biases, and look beyond them. If people want to exclude someone for, say, his or her political views, they need to say that and stand up for what they believe and the message that sends to the team. They must have the courage of their individual convictions when it comes to the good of the team and organization, and ask: Who is this person, and are they the right fit for our team? And if the answer is no, then the blackball is a way for them to say so, free of judgment from their peers. This is not about drama. It's a test of inclusiveness. It's about letting your people have authentic influence on things that directly impact them. And that requires a culture that values the following attributes:

▼ Listening
▼ Vulnerability

▼ Trust

▼ Alignment

All these qualities are essential for sustaining hero cultures. But none can be sustained without the kind of relationships the next-generation talent you want to attract demands during a time when they can basically choose where they want to work.

BLACKBALLING AND RELATIONSHIPS

The first time I used the blackball was when a person I knew approached us about being a Hero Club member. Our team screens all applications for the club, and I knew this gentleman had done some, shall we say, unheroic stuff in the past. I wasn't sure of the details, and nothing I had heard immediately disqualified him. Still, we're an intimate and open organization; I needed to know if he fit with what we're doing. I wasn't going to Goober this guy without checking with the team and getting more facts.

Then he told me he had worked with one of my employees in the past. I immediately went to her and asked for more details. She fumbled a bit, looking for the right words. She mentioned an email she had that could better explain what she was talking about, but at that moment merely said their relationship had been "awkward." I was confused. Had they been a couple? Was it sexual harassment? What was the deal? I called a team meeting—the whole team that runs that part of the business, because we all had a stake in decisions like these—and asked, "What happened?"

The floodgates opened—not tears, but a full-on tirade that I can't repeat here in case there are children present. When she finished, I looked at the rest of the team and asked, "What should we do? It's our decision. He sounds unethical. He took advantage of vendors, brought in family members, cut out other people—just not good."

The team wanted to know more before making the call. We didn't doubt what we'd heard, but decisions like these require due diligence to avoid knee-jerk reactions. There's always two sides to every story. Which one did we feel was right?

I went online and showed the team what this person's business does. We looked at the complaints about customers and vendors being preyed on due to their lack of sophistication. Not nice, but not illegal. There was no sign that this person or his company had much Hero Intensity, but maybe he wanted to join the club so he could learn to do things better. Besides, he couldn't prey on us the same way. If he wanted to do business with people in The Hero Club, it would have to be win-win, or the other members would throw him out. But I reminded the team that the club relied on us to screen potential applicants for a good fit.

"So we don't want to sign the person if they don't meet certain criteria and fit. What do we do?" The team looked at me. This had crossed over into uncomfortable territory. I broke the silence: "Here's the deal. Everybody gets a blackball. Our values say we treat our people like family, and we all have to feel comfortable welcoming someone to the family. If you don't feel the fit is right, you can use your blackball. You just have to have the courage of your convictions, because once you blackball, only you can take it back."

> *Relationships must be more handshake*
> *than hashtag.*

My employee who had worked with the applicant previously blackballed him. I was glad she did. If she hadn't, I would have. This was clearly a member we did not feel good about. But I didn't want her to be a Goober and worry about what others thought but to think about how she felt as part of this team and organization, consider what message her decision sent either way, and have the courage to act. I wanted her not simply to understand but to feel the power of the blackball, realize her genuine influence over this choice, and live with it. This was her mirror moment, and she passed!

A blackball might sound antithetical to real relationships, but they are actually a measurement of just how deeply you care about the culture of your organization and the people who work there. You spend as much time with these people as you do with your actual family. You need to connect with them and feel confident that the people you welcome will have that same connection. Relationships in a hero company are not transactional but by definition *relational*—they are first and foremost about connections between people, not between people and whatever you're selling. A paycheck is a transaction, too: You pay people to show up and do their jobs; you cannot pay them to care or have a relationship with you. Relationships, like cultures, are built, not decreed, and anything that needs building requires work—not only laying the foundation but laboring every day after that to make them grow. They must be maintained if you want them to thrive. And all that must happen authentically, or there will be consequences for your Hero Intensity.

But don't just take my word for it. In 2016, *Harvard Business Review* published the article "A 10-Year Study Reveals What Great Executives Know and Do" by Ron Carucci. A longitudinal study of leadership based on 2,700 interviews and using IBM Watson's analysis tools used "rigorous statistical analysis (including more than 90 regression analyses) to isolate the skills of the top-performing executives" to find what separated the "best of the best." The result was "four highly correlated dimensions," and the fourth really stood out from the rest: "They form deep, trusting relationships." Not because I agree, but because the study said it mattered more than any of the other three dimensions: "It was no surprise that of the four dimensions, relational failure led to the quickest demise among second-best executives. While exceptional executives led with a humble confidence that graciously extended care to others, second-best executives were inclined to manage perceptions, creating the illusion of collaboration while masking self-interested motives."

That is exactly why the blackball works as a tool of inclusion, not exclusion: You can't use it to avoid people or take the easy way out. There are no hidden agendas, no ass covering, no reputation management. No Goobers. Everyone shows their true colors, so to speak. The team and its leaders can then decide how to handle it, hopefully with honest, open, energetic communication built on strong existing relationships and the four attributes I mentioned at the start of this chapter.

Those also happen to be the attributes most mentioned by Hero Club members and other executives I spoke to when it comes to what is essential to sustain hero leadership and cultures: listening, vulnerability, trust, and alignment. Let's look at what I mean by each of them.

LISTENING

Years ago, I was in a business where we were shipping product constantly to get things out on time: "Get the stuff out the door so we can make revenue and meet our quotas *now*." With our Operational Excellence seemingly hanging in the balance, we did what we were told. We forgot about our dedication to quality and our promise to do the best for our customers. We also forgot about what it was doing to our people, from the top of the organization to the floor. Concerns about what was going on were acknowledged, but never pursued. Head down, pedal to the metal, nothing to see here.

We've all lost our way like this at some point. The question is, does anyone have the courage to speak up, and will anyone listen before it brings the culture and the company down? Our company culture had been good up to this point. We were a Good Co. But no one was listening to our people anymore. We were now Bottom Liners, and if we kept going, we would soon be sliding toward Zero.

Then we had a company meeting with the CEO, and I watched as the senior leaders turned on their people and told the CEO what they thought he wanted to hear. They spoke about how great things were going and how everyone was stepping up. That's when one of our people—an hourly worker—had the courage to speak up. He said things were not great. We were breaking our brand promise and cheating our customers: "We're not doing the right things, and we might be putting a product out that is not quite ready or not checked for quality in packaging and shipping. Is that OK if I raise my hand and say, 'No, that is not acceptable'?"

The senior leaders were shocked, and I wondered what the CEO was going to say. He had to be surprised, given this was the first he had heard of this. I wondered: Would he be willing to listen, *really* listen to what this person had to say? "Absolutely, that's OK," our CEO said, looking around the room at everyone but focusing hard on the leaders. "Does that mean we are going to lose revenue and make customers unhappy short term? Yes. But we are going to fix this. And in the end, we will get a better customer for any we lose, because we did the right thing."

Our CEO was right. The company took a hit but recovered within the year to achieve record revenue and profits and may have even jumped back to Good Co. and toward Hero. And what if we hadn't recovered? Well, at least it wouldn't be because we failed to do the right thing and listened.

> *If you can't ask questions before speaking,*
> *you aren't really interested in listening.*

What can you do to listen? Well, start by doing what that hourly worker had the guts to do: *Speak up and ask questions.* Get your butt out of your chair, walk over to a desk, and ask a question to someone's face. Not a demand, like, "Where's the report I asked for?" or a yes/no question. One that opens people up and requires a thoughtful answer—the more personal and less work-driven, the better. Anything that shows you care about their well-being. Maybe try to find out one thing you don't know about them:

▼ What did you do this weekend?
▼ Who is that in the picture on your desk?
▼ Where do you like to eat dinner when you go out?

Then listen to the answer and *ask at least two more follow-up questions before saying anything about you.* This is what John Greco, CEO of Greco Associates, called "active listening" in Chapter 4 and led to his team coming together to win. But it only works if you stop thinking about yourself and genuinely care about others—and let them ask questions of you, too.

A big part of listening is asking questions to understand. You *want* your people to do that, so you need to model this behavior, which is why I am always happy for my people to ask good, thoughtful questions when we launch a new program so they can execute better. The more you do that, the more you not only show your people you care but also connect and begin to form real relationships with them. When an employee feels that connection, it makes them want to work harder to serve you and deliver better results. By listening to others, you also learn to put yourself in the other person's shoes to ask bigger and more important questions, like: What does this potential customer want? How can I help my boss do more? What is the other party in our joint venture or partnership trying to accomplish?

Of course, questioning can cross a line. Leaders can never tolerate questions designed to undermine authority, prove what they don't know, or make excuses. I am intolerant when my people keep questioning why the company is doing what we are doing and attacking it, as if I didn't consider all sides before making the decision. Any question like that sounds like it's really saying, "Jeff, you know that makes you an idiot, right?" That's the worst kind of entitlement: thinking you know better.

That said, sometimes I am an idiot. I *do* make mistakes even when I believe in my head and heart we are doing the right thing. That's when any leader must do more than listen.

VULNERABILITY

"Every entrepreneur is in that fetal position when they are away from their company too many times. Someone who can rise from that is what a real leader is," Jerry Henley, CEO of Rubicon Capital, told me when we spoke for this book. But I would go one step further: Hero leaders rise from that fetal position to lead *and* let their teams see it all.

That's vulnerability: opening yourself up to others. Hero companies and leaders find strength in that.

That vulnerability takes courage, because so many leaders have been conditioned to believe that vulnerability is synonymous with weakness. Yet it actually strengthens relationships. I mean, how many genuinely strong personal relationships in business and in life can be built on hiding your flaws, bad news, or problems? How many lasted when you hid a betrayal or a mistake? And how many mistakes were forgiven because you showed genuine vulnerability?

Shea Sealy, president and founder of Advanced Building Care, a maintenance and janitorial company, calls this courage to be vulnerable "meekness," because it carries a spiritual significance that too many leaders and organizations of faith often forget: "Do we as leaders and executives readily and frequently acknowledge the accomplishments of others, help them to turn their weaknesses into strengths, and instill confidence within them?" he says. "How do we act or react when we are hurt by the wrongdoings of our employees, clients, and/or competitors? Do we act out of anger and seek revenge, or do we utilize those difficult experiences as both learning and teaching opportunities for ourselves and for others? Jesus Christ demonstrates both his servant and his leadership traits throughout his entire earthly and divine ministries with meekness, 'disciplined response, strong self-restraint, and unwillingness to exert power for personal benefit.' I am fully convinced that it is the greater understanding and development of the attribute of meekness that will truly transform our cultures and ultimately create winning organizations. We will see a dramatic increase in the amount of trustworthy relationships found within and outside our companies,

---

Leaders need to be vulnerable enough to admit
that they make mistakes and don't know all
the answers.

---

and we will better be prepared to handle the inevitable adversities within our organizations."

I love the idea of strength through adversity. Resilience is essential to great leadership and organizations, but you can't show resilience if you don't have the courage to be transparent about problems and mistakes in front of your people. Catherine Monson, CEO of Fastsigns International, understands this link between courage and vulnerability and how it can prevent future problems: "That courage could be anything from running toward the problem to telling your team where you've made a mistake," she says. "We have a management committee meeting every two weeks where all the middle managers and executives are together, and even as the CEO, I need to gather the courage to share mistakes I have made in front of the group. But it has a big impact on everybody, this courage to talk about a problem. It also leads to the courage to be caring when people have problems. The courage to say, 'I don't care what the issue is. We're still going to take care of this employee, whatever it might be.'"

So how are you going to be more vulnerable to strengthen your relationships? Here are some suggestions:

- ▼ Stop thinking you know everything, or stop pretending to
- ▼ Be willing to be challenged and learn—let your team push you
- ▼ Do not see difference as a challenge to your values
- ▼ Be humble enough to admit flaws, not just failures
- ▼ Collaborate and be willing to share credit and success

That last one is especially important. No one I know is successful without others. Maybe those people exist. I'm sure they're lonely, wherever they are. I'm not. I love my team, and I want them to push themselves and push me. In some ways, I have found this vulnerability easier as I get older. I have had far more successes than failures, so I have more confidence in who I am. I'm also less prone to questioning myself than I used to be, worrying whether I'm good enough or second-guessing my decisions. The farther I've gotten in my career, the more I trust myself about what we're doing and how we're doing it. I have also figured out what I want and don't want to do personally.

But that doesn't mean I want that professionally for my team and business. I want my team to be entrepreneurial—to do and see things I don't to grow the business together. That's why my team has the blackball. I need to be vulnerable enough to allow my team that influence—to trust that they might see and feel things I don't and still make the right call for my business, even if it's not what I want or would do. And that's OK. Because I trust them.

TRUST

If you lose the trust of your people, partners, vendors, customers, and community, it's harder than ever to recover it. Things live forever online, and even if your people stop believing the bad stuff, it's still out there for others to find. So how can you maintain that trust in your organization and your professional relationships?

▼ Competency: doing things successfully and efficiently
▼ Sincerity: doing things openly, honestly, and without hypocrisy
▼ Relevancy: being connected to your values and others and living that way

Let's go into each of these a little deeper.

Competency

Many leaders think of competency in terms of Operational Excellence, and that *is* a huge component. But if you think about it solely in those terms, then trust is really just about a paycheck—a transaction. Your people trust the company to pay them for the work they do, and they do what they're told. As I've said before, this isn't necessarily a bad thing; it's just not a Hero thing. After all, strong Operational Excellence in a Bottom Liner usually means a successful company in terms of revenue.

But there are different measures of success today that fall more on the Hero Intensity side, and that's where the other part of competency lies: *How well you treat others, from coaching them to empowering them to be the best they can be, both for themselves and your company.* A Bottom Liner may not see the importance of this, but when the competition for the best talent is fierce, a big payday to join a culture that cares only about the numbers might not best serve a company, especially when it comes to recruiting Millennials and others looking for a purpose beyond a paycheck.

Sincerity

The easiest way to break trust with your people and kill a hero culture is of course not living your values: saying one thing and doing another. But you don't need to be dishonest to be insincere; people only need to *feel* you lack sincerity, especially if you are telling partial truths and not coming clean or not telling them all they need to know. I'll say that again for good measure: This lack of sincerity is felt most often in apologies that leaders and organizations make for their mistakes, not only in how they sound but also in the tangible actions they take.

The hero gold standard for this, in my opinion, is Johnson & Johnson in 1982, when someone was poisoning its Tylenol products with cyanide, killing seven people. The company skipped the mea culpas and went straight to action, putting customer safety over cost and saving countless lives by stopping production and recalling *every one* of its Tylenol products, at a cost of $100 million. Interestingly, Johnson & Johnson is also a good Zero example. In 2010, it failed to take corrective action, knowingly selling children's Tylenol products that could contain metal particles and had to pay $25 million in federal fines, still do the recall, and advise consumers to stop using the medicine.

Johnson & Johnson fell from Hero to Zero. What will you do? Will you do the right thing and be transparent about everything you can? Ignore the problem? Cover it up? As I write this book, multiple organizations—Facebook over the use of customer data, Michigan State over the abuse of young gymnasts, Tesla over worker safety, and Nestlé over the use of child labor—are showing the perils of a lack of transparency when it comes to admitting mistakes, as we learn more about what these companies did not tell us.

How little do you have to value transparency, let alone others, to do that? You might think you are too big or too powerful for it to cost you, but that's when heroes start to fall. It doesn't take long to become irrelevant these days.

Relevancy

When you lose or lack relevancy, you lose both talent and customers, and thus Operational Excellence. Too many times we focus on the customer side when it comes to relevancy. We trot out tales of BlackBerry, Oldsmobile, and Kodak and their failures to adapt and innovate. We should! They are important lessons. But that same lack of adaptation and innovation often costs companies in the workplace first, as they try to shore up their Operational Excellence. They ignore new opportunities and keep selling the same stuff. They move jobs overseas as revenues decline. They fail to invest in new people and partners to reach new and different customers. What these companies often fail to see is that you lose relevancy in the workplace long before the marketplace, because leaders and organizations see their relationships with each other as irrelevant. There's no room for trust in that kind of culture. No expectation of reciprocity beyond the transaction of a paycheck for work performed.

ALIGNMENT

I love this quote from Lee Iacocca: "I'm constantly amazed by the number of people who can't seem to control their own schedules. Over the years, I've had many executives come to me and say with pride: 'Boy, last year I worked so hard that I didn't take any vacation.' It's actually nothing to be proud of. I always feel like responding: 'You dummy. You mean to tell me that you can take responsibility for an $80 million project and you can't plan two weeks out of the year to go off with your family and have some fun?'"

Iacocca understood the need for balance in the workplace. Today, the need for a different kind of balance has emerged to create more hero companies and leaders: the need for alignment. A 2016 study of Millennials by Deloitte found them loyal to companies that support their own career and life ambitions. In fact, when Millennials do feel this way, they tend to stay longer at those companies than the previous generation, because they trust those companies and their leaders to value their goals and purpose as individuals and as part of a team. They believe their goals can align with the goals of the companies and still get results so everyone grows. This is something every leader at any business should be attuned to in forming relationships.

Are the values of the people who work for you aligned with the values of the company? Do you share each other's goals?

Too often, leaders confuse this alignment with conformity. They say "We align our values," but what they mean is "You obey my values."

BE A HERO: YOU DON'T NEED A BLACKBALL TO TEST RELATIONSHIPS

This is a good exercise to see how you will fare when your people and others you connect with take the Hero Assessment. It tests the foundation of your relationships with them.

Have your people rate you from 1 to 10, with 1 being lowest and 10 being highest, on the following qualities:

▼ How well you listen and ask questions

▼ How vulnerable you are

▼ Your commitment to trust when it comes to competency, sincerity, and relevancy

▼ Your reciprocity: the alignment between your goals and theirs

Now rate yourself on the same things. Gather all the scores but yours and average them. Now compare them to yours: Where do they match up, and where are they lower or higher? Why? Show the differing scores to your people and ask them the same questions.

> *Let your people find their "call" and a personal sense of meaning in what they do by serving you.*

And that is partly true: I see people as individuals, but they must serve my values and vision to help the company's culture stay strong, and I hope they see their own values and vision in mine. That, however, does not preclude me from letting them be themselves as they serve my vision and collaborate with others. People are your greatest asset—their differences are strengths to be cultivated, not forced to conform.

Put it this way: So many leaders are willing to be flexible and understanding in their personal relationships. Why can't they be that way in their professional relationships as well? Why are the same people lumps of coal in the workplace and diamonds in their living rooms? Why do we think they need to give in and give up to us—even when it comes to giving back to others?

That brings us to the final stop on our hero journey.

CHAPTER 16

HEROES GIVE *MORE,* NOT JUST *BACK*

Rob Ryan, founder of The Hero Club, launched Ascend Communications in 1989 and grew it to more than $2 billion in revenue over the next ten years. In 1999, Lucent Technologies acquired Ascend for approximately $20 billion in a deal that stood as the largest technology merger ever until Microsoft bought LinkedIn for $26.2 billion in 2016. The deal made Rob wealthy beyond anything he had ever imagined, but he changed little about his life. He lived in the same house, drove the same car with its "Ascend1" license plates, and ate lunch at his favorite cafe. In fact, the cafe changed more than he did in the days following the merger: Scenes from *Mrs. Doubtfire* starring Robin Williams were being filmed there, and crowds formed regularly hoping to get a glimpse of the star, which is what Rob at first assumed was happening when he stepped outside after eating lunch one day. Then, squinting past the afternoon sun, Rob realized he recognized more than a few faces in the crowd. That's when they all started to applaud and race forward to shake *his* hand.

Here's why: Rob believed in sharing the wealth. When he sold Ascend, he didn't just take the money and run; he set aside 10 percent for *all* the people who made it possible. That's *$2 billion*, not just for executives but also janitors, night watchmen, secretaries, and others. All of them became instant millionaires. In fact, the merger set a record for the most millionaires created in a single day. Those were the people surrounding Rob at the café: employees who knew his regular lunch plans and waited by his car with the signature license plates for him to come out. One by one, they stepped up to tell him how he had changed their lives overnight: They could afford college for their kids, an operation for a loved one, to pay off that mortgage with the absurd interest rate . . . the list went on of the dreams they could now realize.

That story makes me weepy every time I tell it. It also makes me think of the old Steve Martin comedy bit "You Can Be a Millionaire" (and never pay taxes). First, get a million dollars. Then, when the tax man shows up, tell him you forgot. Those men and women of Ascend worked hard and were paid fairly, but I'm pretty sure they never thought the first part of Martin's joke could become true. I'm positive, however, they were delighted that Rob never said, "Oops, I forgot about the others who got me here."

Hamdi Ulukaya didn't forget either. In fact, he didn't even wait to cash out before he laid the foundation to do the same thing Rob Ryan did. In 2016, the same year I took over The Hero Club and started telling Rob's story, Ulukaya created 2,000 potential millionaires in the full-time employees at his company: the $1.5 billion yogurt giant Chobani. According to *USA Today*, Ulukaya told those employees that they would "receive shares worth up to 10 percent of the company's value when it goes public or is sold. 'This isn't a gift,' Ulukaya said in a letter to [them]. 'It's a mutual promise to work together with a shared purpose and responsibility. To continue to create something special and of lasting value.'"

Like Rob Ryan, Ulukaya saw the power and promise of recognizing ordinary people and seeing them as individuals to be empowered—not commodities to be used and discarded for profit. A Kurdish man who emigrated to the United States from Turkey in 1994, he used the values he learned growing up in a family that farmed cows and herded sheep to create a shared purpose among all his people. Why? Because they had a stake—and he had their backs. Together, they transformed the culture at Chobani by motivating each other to help themselves and the company be better, grow, and win. As Ulukaya told *Inc.*, "Among shepherds, what's respected most is people's values. You provide, you protect." That's why he has also taken steps to honor his own immigrant roots and the entrepreneurial opportunity America afforded him when he took over an abandoned yogurt factory in upstate New York in 2005. Ulukaya has courageously urged businesses to hire more immigrants and has welcomed refugees the federal government has sent to work at the world's largest yogurt factory he built in Twin Falls, Idaho. Despite the current anti-immigrant political climate, he remains steadfast in his push for inclusivity with a workforce that is now made up of more than 30 percent immigrants and refugees.

Long ago, I heard a speaker say if you *give give give* you *get get get*, and the time has come for that idea on a heroic scale. What Rob Ryan and Hamdi Ulukaya have in common at their core is they understand the power of not just giving back but giving more—doing more for others than you ever thought possible, both in terms of philanthropy and how you share the wealth.

Will you remember to give back and give more? Or, rather, *when* will you remember to give back and give more? You need to empower your people and transform not just your culture but your organization, the community it is a part of, and the world it touches.

GIVING BACK AND GIVING MORE TO YOUR PEOPLE

To be clear, anyone and any business that chooses to give back and transparently delivers on that promise gets a baseline salute. Only people and companies with no philanthropic component or who fail to deliver on their promise are Zeroes. That said, can you think of a single company that does not give back in some way? Pick up any package in a supermarket or big box store, look at the social media feeds and websites of your favorite brands, check out the annual reports of the companies you invest in and the one you work for . . . it won't take long to find something about giving back.

I love that so many are doing well by doing good, and there are plenty of cool companies doing great things for others with the money they make. But there are far too many to list here that meet that standard, which is why that only gets them into Good Co. territory. Of course, many fall short of that. Most organizations—and many people—give passively by simply cutting a check. This kind of giving just makes you a Wannabe. Decades ago, it might have raised your Hero Intensity more, but today, it shows only a modicum of care.

In fact, some companies I looked into had no idea where the money they donated to a charity went. They didn't even check to see if the charity had high ratings on sites like Charity Navigator (https://www. charitynavigator.org) or CharityWatch (https://www.charitywatch. org), independent evaluators that rate charities on things like what percentage of funds raised goes to the people they are trying to help and what percentage goes to fundraising and salaries.

But even if their charities of choice did have high ratings, leaders and organizations have to push well beyond this kind of giving to get into the Good Co. range. To me, cutting a check or sponsoring something without any meaningful and sustainable connection—no matter how big the check is—is the equivalent of tossing coins into a homeless person's cup as you walk by without stopping. You think that makes you a hero? I don't care how many coins you toss from your company's proverbial pocket. If that's what makes you feel better about yourself, I feel sorry for your lack of a soul. You'll never know the joy of looking the people you're helping in the eye. But hey, at least you gave something!

I'm talking about giving *more*, which means giving of yourself until it hurts—until *you feel it*.

Hero giving means doing this all the time as a part of how you live—so much so that it is inseparable from who you are and what your brand stands for. That's why Heroes constantly push themselves and their people to do more—to *be* more than just Bottom Liners, Wannabes, and Good Cos. To be accountable to something greater than themselves. It's so rooted in their identities as leaders and the culture of their organizations that they can't separate it from everything else they do.

Think of hero giving like exercise. When you vigorously exercise— really push yourself every day to stay strong and healthy—you can feel the difference. When you give like a hero, you can feel it too, no matter what kind of shape you're in. Anything less, and you are not getting your hero heart rate up. And if you're "out of shape" in your giving or never push yourself to do more, you won't feel much at all.

You don't need to have millions or billions like Rob Ryan and Hamdi Ulukaya to achieve this. Giving back isn't measured by the

---

BE A HERO: GIVE BACK OR GIVE MORE?

Take a hard look at how much you, your organization, and your people give back to charity and your community. Write it all out.

- ▼ Put a "P" by everything that is passive giving (meaning it happens with very little time or effort on anyone's part).

- ▼ Put an "A" by everything that is active giving (meaning it requires time and effort).

- ▼ Now divide the P's and A's into one column each, step back, and ask yourself: Which do you feel strongest about and why? Which do your people feel strongest about and why? How can you give more to those A's and those you feel strongest about?

> *Give until it hurts; no pain, no hero gain.*

number of zeroes at the end. That's about scale, not generosity. Say a person down on his luck approaches two people he knows and says he needs some cash for some food. One opens his wallet and gives him $20; the other gives him $10. Which friend was more generous? In dollar value, the one who gave $20. But what if that person had $100 in his wallet and the person who gave $10 only had $10?

Are you giving all you can to the people who need it? Are you choosing to give more and be the hero your people need you to be in terms of the way you reward your people and your charitability to others?

For those of you who think this is where Jeff rails against CEO salaries, you're wrong. I don't like the fact that the salaries of many CEOs are hundreds if not thousands of times higher than their average employees' wages. And I certainly take issue with those companies that compensate their CEOs millions (and the CEOs who seek millions in compensation) when they are losing money, laying off hundreds of workers, and going bankrupt. But if those companies believe their CEOs deserve the money because they are responsible for gains that exceed expectations for Wall Street, shareholders, and/or investors? That doesn't make them evil, just not heroes—and we need heroes.

For example, McDonald's CEO Steve Easterbrook earned almost $22 million in 2017, more than 3,101 times the company's median employee. The company defended it by saying Easterbrook grew the company by $36 billion. If McDonald's thinks it's getting a 1,714 times return on its CEO, that makes it a pretty great investment for a Bottom Liner company that cares only about Operational Excellence. I just don't see any Hero Intensity in that answer, especially as the company fights raising wages for its workers—the ones who most need to be given more.

As for Easterbrook himself, his Hero Intensity as a leader is not diminished by taking what he was offered but by his values and how he values others. CEOs and other senior leaders are not anti-heroes just because they make a lot of money. It's what they do with their power and that money to empower themselves *and* others. It's how they make the workplace better for everyone, not just its C-suite and Wall Street. Consider Nido Qubein, the president of High Point University (who figured prominently in Chapter 10). He is one of the highest-paid college presidents in the United States, earning $2.9 million a year in recent reports. But *The Chronicle of Higher Education* noted in 2016 he had committed at least $10 million back to the university to make it a better place—something reflected in the hero culture of the school.

McDonald's made a choice, and it's not the hero way. They bet you care more about paying less than $1 for a burger than what the person cooking it or handing it to you makes. Are they right? What if it was your son or daughter back there? In a time when we are bombarded with stories about stubbornly stagnant wages in a growing economy, organizations and their leaders—not to mention their customers— need to think about what they are giving back to the people at the bottom. Too many hourly and low-wage/salaried workers, as well as young professionals and their families, are priced out of homes, apartments, and entire cities and regions. Too many people have lost faith in organizations to care about them beyond the bottom line and give them opportunities to earn more and grow—or even just live lives in which they can spend time with their families and not have to drive an Uber for six hours after work to pay rent and buy food.

So don't call people who want you to give more entitled without looking at yourself in the mirror first, and don't say that you suffered when you started out, so they should too. Really? You think shared pain is the only way? The best people, which is to say most people, don't want money for nothing. They just want to be rewarded for performance and given an opportunity for growth and maybe a chance to share in the wealth. Sure, they can dream of the scale of Rob Ryan and Hamdi Ulukaya, but is it so hard to give more so your people feel they have more stake in the success of the organization to help you and them win?

It's your choice: to do and give more for your people or do more for your bottom line and Wall Street. So pick a side!

Think you are already giving all you can? Ask these questions of yourself and your leaders that have nothing to do with compensation. If you can't answer these questions easily, what makes you think you are giving more to your people anywhere else?

▼ How do you go out of your way every day to show gratitude to your people—even in a simple way, like a handshake for a job well done?

▼ How do you spend time with your people to coach them on how to maximize their potential and share your experience?

▼ When was the last time you brought small gifts of appreciation for a job well done or just a simple handwritten thank-you next to an unexpected coffee delivery on a brutal day? (Triple shot for me, please.)

Now let's go to the other extreme and consider Alan and Eric Barnhart of Barnhart Crane & Rigging, which provides heavy lifting and transportation services across the country. They not only refused to take a higher salary than the average middle class income in their hometown of Memphis, Tennessee, and gave much of the company's profits to charity ($100 million over 30 years), but in 2007 they gave the whole company to the National Christian Foundation. According to *Philanthropy Magazine*, 50 percent of all company earnings are donated immediately to charity, and the other 50 percent are used to grow the business (including cost of living increases for the employees).

I'm not an evangelical Christian, but you don't have to be to smile at the depth of the Barnharts' belief in stewardship. All hero companies and their leaders hear the call to do more—to feel what they give and get so much more by making it meaningful to them and those they connect to and serve.

THE CALL TO HERO GIVING

Many companies do some or all of the following things and more to raise their Hero Intensity: matching gifts, in-kind donations, hosting and attending fundraisers, and performing pro bono work for nonprofits. But that kind of giving back is still not raising their

Hero Intensity—it's not hearing the hero call to give more. That's what 1-800-Flowers.com CEO Chris McCann and his brother Jim, who founded the company, did when they heard the call. In 2015, their family launched Smile Farms, a 501(c)3 organization that provides meaningful work in agricultural settings to individuals with developmental disabilities—something deeply personal to Chris and Jim. Its success not only raised the company's Hero Intensity but its Operational Excellence as well.

"My brother and I were talking about how we do a lot of giving and cause-related marketing to wonderful and deserving groups," Chris says. "But we really should have one that we kind of get behind—that our company could really make a connection to. One that is closely associated with our brand and the people in the company can touch, feel, and be part of, more than just knowing that the company is contributing to it. We were trying to figure out what that was and meeting with a couple of different national charities when we realized we had one in our midst."

Chris and Jim's brother, Kevin, who is developmentally disabled, lives in a group home in Long Island. The brothers had helped build a greenhouse there and it was going gangbusters, employing his brother along with 30 more developmentally disabled adults. They grow plants and produce and sell them wholesale and retail. Chris and Jim saw the importance that the job had to their brother's self-worth. It impacted him and their family deeply. So when the person who ran the greenhouse at the home said he had more people who needed jobs and asked for help, Chris and Jim launched Smile Farms.

As of 2018, Smile Farms has seven locations and employs more than 100 people growing plants and flowers for 1-800-Flowers.com and food for restaurateurs like Tom Colicchio. More important, they are valuing others who tend to be the *least* valued people when it comes to jobs. "Now we're providing jobs to people who usually don't have a chance," Chris says. "There's an 80 percent unemployment rate among people with developmental disabilities. We're trying to change that. We also discovered just how many of our employees have developmentally disabled people in their lives. We are touching their lives and hearts, too. We built an organization to help others that is closely tied to our brand, but equally important, something that is impacting the lives of every one of our employees."

That kind of impact doesn't just look good on a spreadsheet or in marketing materials; it feels good every day. It links the bottom line to call and purpose, which is what the Hero Factor is all about.

For members of The Hero Club and beyond, this call and purpose manifests itself in different ways. For Christopher Cumby, founder of Think Bold, Be Bold Ventures, giving more extends not just to how we treat others but also to care for ourselves: "What's most important is our health, our well-being, if you want to call it that. Am I taking care of myself the way I need to? Does my workplace have resources that I can tap into? Are they giving me insight on how to take care of myself nutritionally? Can they give me some ideas on exercise? Will it pay my gym fee? I mean, let's face it. It's a small price to pay for the benefits. If you have people who are taking care of themselves, they're going to show up with a better attitude that allows commitment and connection."

> ### *How do you give more to your people,*
> ### *your community, and beyond?*

For other Hero Club members, there's a deeply spiritual side to that call akin to the Barnharts'. For example, Derek Tippins, CEO of app development company Nyoobe, told me he learned this as he launched his new company and went beyond where his giving had gone before: "If giving back can be a win-win for somebody in our team, then that's great. As a new startup and as a Christian, I'm learning every day what we can do beyond normal tithing stuff. After a hurricane ripped through the South, four guys and I drove semis with supplies down there, and it felt really good. It touched these guys and me, who are working men—$50,000-to-$60,000-a-year type guys. We talked about how it will be nice when Nyoobe can pay them to do this full time." That kind of hero pledge means more to me than Mark Zuckerberg pledging to give it all away when he cashes out.

Ask yourself:

▼ What are you willing to sacrifice *now* for the greater good of valuing others?

▼ How far are you willing to go to make an impact on the people around you and the people and communities you care about?

And remember: Just like inclusive leadership does not need to compromise Operational Excellence and growth, neither does giving back to your people and your community. In fact, it can go hand-in-hand as it does for Belden, a 100-plus-year-old company in Richmond, Indiana. Belden makes cables consumers and businesses use to connect peripherals to the internet. According to a story on National Public Radio's *Morning Edition*, Richmond is a company town and Belden is its company, deeply dedicated to its employees and community. Generations of Richmond families have worked for it, and business was booming in 2018. That boom presented a problem. It takes 450 people to run the factory to meet demand, and talent was scarce. For the second time in two years, Belden could not find enough qualified workers to fill its open positions. One of the biggest reasons was one of the biggest problems facing America today: opioid addiction. An enormous percentage of the already small talent pool available in the area was failing the company's drug test.

This time, however, Belden didn't just throw up its hands and miss its sales targets. It bucked the status quo and did something about it: It created a pilot program that offered drug treatment to applicants who failed a drug test and a job when they completed it. If that's not giving back with the highest Hero Intensity and Operational Excellence *and* raising your Hero Factor through the roof, I don't know what is. Will the Belden program work? At the time of the NPR story, 17 people had entered the one-to-four-month program. Costs will exceed $5,000 per participant (all paid by Belden). But with demand for its products steady, the labor shortage showing no signs of stopping, and with a third of Belden workers hitting retirement soon, giving more may be the only way to keep growing and make sure it is there for its people and community in the long run. "We've been in his community since 1928," Leah Tate, Belden's vice president of human resources, told NPR. "We have families of families that have worked in this plant and for this company—so the Richmond community is extremely important to Belden."

Think about Belden and other stories that make you feel great when you read them, and imagine having that feeling yourself, no matter how much you make. Consider Jim Estill, the CEO of Danby, an appliance company in Canada, who put up $1.1 million to save 58 Syrian refugee families. Or celebrity chef José Andrés and his team, who took weeks off to serve more than 3 million meals to people in Puerto Rico at a fraction of the cost a Zero company charged FEMA and then failed to deliver.

None of these people did what they did to get media attention. First and foremost, they did it because it was the right thing to do. Most of the time, heroes like these don't want attention. What I loved in the Barnharts' story was that Alan didn't even want to talk about what he had done. According to the magazine, "he started giving interviews about his philanthropy only after others convinced him to do so." This is the exact opposite of the kind of virtue signaling that too many companies deploy these days.

Virtue signaling is expressing certain sentiments to demonstrate your good character and moral correctness. Some companies do it wrong: through self-congratulatory ads on TV or as a public relations maneuver to cover up or to try and undo the bad things they have done. Some do it as a calculated business move: to make sure the people they want to attract as customers and employees know their heart is in the right place and to inspire others to act. Some do a little of both. Either way, the fact that virtue signaling has become such a familiar concept is evidence of just how many companies are giving back and are trying to get attention and credit for it. Subaru and MassMutual have made it part of major advertising campaigns, the latter in an ad it spent millions to air before the Super Bowl. The goal may be to raise the firm's Operational Excellence by attracting more customers, but are they raising or lowering their Hero Intensity at the same time? The answer is unclear.

What *is* clear is that hero companies that give more are choosing to rethink traditional templates for corporate philanthropy and the nature of giving back. They are measuring impact not in dollars but in how it makes their people feel and how it connects them to one another within the company and in the community. They have learned that giving back is not a mask for corrupt cultures but part of the movement to create cultures that are accepting and inspiring to all people.

This can be measured in actions large and small, such as allowing offices and stores in different regions to tailor their giving to the needs of those communities. (One location may be dealing with a homeless problem, another may need more playground equipment for kids, yet another might need people to clean up its public areas.) But the future of Hero giving goes beyond this to allow your people to influence how the organization gives back, which brings this book back to where we started this hero journey: the American entrepreneurial spirit.

GIVING OTHERS THE POWER TO GIVE

When Derek Tippins told me about him and his team driving down to help victims of a hurricane and creating a standing disaster relief team, he also told me it inspired this about the team that works directly with him: "I told them instead of me and the app giving money to charity, we're going to take the money that we're going to give and divide it up equally between things that are important to each of us," he says. "Whatever's important to you, that's your baby as a representative of Nyoobe for that company." The Barnharts have done the same thing, according to *Philanthropy Magazine*: "A group of 55 employees and spouses decides where to distribute half of the money made every year by Barnhart Crane & Rigging. Each employee in the group—which is dubbed GROVE, God's Resources Operating Very Effectively—develops a relationship with one or two grant recipients, researching their effectiveness and vetting their requests."

You don't need to evoke or even believe in God to do that for your employees. Salesforce, Subaru, Daimler, General Mills, and others have secular cultures of employee-centered and employee-directed giving. The companies provide the time or the funds, and their people determine either individually or by collective vote where that time and money goes. Is there a limit to this? Of course. You can't allow giving more to get in the way of Operational Excellence. You have to say no sometimes. Remember: Too much give and not enough get, and you end up a Struggling Do-Gooder.

But most companies and leaders don't do this because they *don't hear the call to be other-directed and value all people as individuals in everything they do*, especially when it comes to empowering them to give more. You want your people to be entrepreneurial in all they do, and that includes supporting them in what they care most about when it comes to helping others.

So don't just encourage it—mandate it! Yes, it's hard and messy and complicated, but it's real and brings out "all the feels," as the young folk say.

I can't say what it will look like for you—what call you will hear, how to answer it, and how you will strive to give more. I will repeat what I have said from the start: Giving more, like everything else that makes up your Hero Factor, is a choice. But while the choice to give more may be one of the last choices you can make in this book, none is more important to creating the next generation of heroes and keeping your hero journey going. Giving isn't just living—it's what makes you feel alive inside and out. It's the end *and* the beginning of the Hero Factor and beats deep in the heart of every hero. Give back or give more: The choice is yours.

QUESTIONS ON HOW YOU VALUE OTHERS

As you prepare to take the Hero Factor Assessment again or for the first time, consider these questions about how you value others:

▼ What's the *feel* of the culture of your organization? How do you see and feel it reflected in the mood of your people and the way they work?

▼ How inclusive are you of different perspectives *and* people—and what are you doing to be more inclusive?

▼ Do you see your people as commodities or individuals? What has more value: your people or the sale?

▼ How do you show you care about others?

▼ When faced with serious change, how do you value your people? How do you empower and coach them to lead and serve through the change process?

▼ Do you allow your people to lead and create—to have the independence to pursue opportunities you don't see so you can not only know what you don't know but also benefit from learning it?

▼ Does your culture have psychological safety for all, or is it an echo chamber?

▼ Are the values of the people who work for you aligned with the values of the company? Do you share each other's goals?

▼ Do you listen to your people and allow them the opportunity to influence how the work is done, creating an environment of trust?

▼ Do you and thus your organization confuse conformity with alignment?

▼ Do you and thus your organization confuse weakness with vulnerability?

▼ Are you and thus your organization transparent in all you do?

▼ Are you and thus your organization decisive and calm through the chaos?

▼ How do you give back to your people, your community, and beyond aside from cutting a check?

▼ Do you and your organization direct your giving, or do your people have influence?

HEROES STEP UP
WHAT WILL YOUR LEGACY BE?

L ouis L'Amour is my favorite author of all time. I've read and own every one of his 100-plus novels and short story collections. Not only do I own them, most are signed first editions. I even have multiple copies of my favorites. Why? Because I can. I started collecting when I was a kid, never stopped, and never want to. And I'm hardly alone. L'Amour died in 1988, yet *every one of his books* is still in print. There are more than 200 million of them in circulation. Forty-five of them have been made into movies.

L'Amour wrote mostly Westerns, and the cowboy in me loves those the most. Pretty much every book starts with an evil act being committed: a school or town terrorized, for example, its people killed, menaced, or kidnapped by a villain and his henchmen. A hero rises from the chaos that follows. He (always a he) leaves on a mission for justice. He rides his horse for days through harsh terrain. He hunts for food. He deploys survival methods that demonstrate his resilience and ability to innovate. He ponders life. Finally, against all odds, despite grave danger, and at great personal sacrifice, he rescues the hostages and defeats the villains.

Yes, it's a formula, but a timeless one. L'Amour understood the power of heroes who were not superhuman but ordinary men of extraordinary character who heard the call to leadership. It wasn't the heroes' ranches that got burned or their children who were kidnapped. They were usually loners. But still, they couldn't abide what the bad guys were doing to everybody else. So L'Amour's heroes did all this selflessly in the service of others—both the people they knew and those they never would but who thanks to them would never have to experience the villains' brand of evil. Calm amidst the chaos, they stepped up to be strong and protect the weak—to strive in the name of justice to build a better tomorrow for all.

Simply put, L'Amour's books are about the heroes I want to believe in and want to believe I can be. That we *all* want to believe in and believe we can be.

Because we can. The age of heroes needs us. It's time to step up. No more excuses.

Unlike L'Amour's heroes, you don't need to be a man or a loner to have the Hero Factor. If you want to be a hero, you just need to fight through the naysayers, obstructionists, biases, status quo, and limitations (real and perceived). You probably won't need to hunt for your food (though I wish I could more often than I do), and you definitely don't need to throw a literal punch to knock out evil. You just need to make the choice to step up. To hear the call to hero leadership.

The call is deep and powerful. Expect it to move you in ways you might not have expected when you answer it. Since I did, I find myself asking more and more, "What have I really done to be the best person I can be? What will be the legacy I leave behind?" Sure, I have made money, had fun, and taken care of my family. I have followed my heart and dreams and realized many of my visions—my north stars—large and small along the way. I will realize many more before I'm done. But there is only one true north star, one overarching purpose for all of us: the one that says, "We share this world with others, and we have a greater purpose than just helping those we know and sharing what we make."

Heroes and aspiring heroes know there's always more they could do. They don't wait to act. They choose the hero side and keep doing the right thing, the good thing, for all people again and again. Remember: Anybody can do something once. What comes next, and what comes after that, as you keep building and sustaining your Hero Factor?

So let me end by asking you the same question I posed in Chapter 1: Are you ready? Ready not only to grow your Operational Excellence and Hero Intensity but also to inspire the next generation of hero leaders to make tomorrow better?

I know the work and sacrifice this takes—the willingness to fight past what is easy and do what's right. I strive to do it every day. For my children. For my children's children. For yours, too. And for the generations beyond. We've had enough of tribalism, shortsightedness, and single-minded absolutes. Your moment of truth is here. Look yourself in the mirror. What do you see? A Hero, a Good Co., a Bottom Liner, a Struggling Do-Gooder, a Wannabe, or a Zero? Is what you see what you want to be? Are those the values you and your organization want to have?

If your answers are yes, great. You do you. If you want to be or stay a Hero, welcome. This isn't another mirror moment. This is your legacy moment. *What will your hero legacy be?* Pick a side, and then get on your horse and ride!

THE **HERO FACTOR** ASSESSMENT

Restating what I said in Part I, the **Hero Factor** of any organization and leader is determined by combining scores from 0-10 on two equally weighted scales all heroes must hold themselves accountable to: **Operational Excellence** and **Hero Intensity**. Thus, the Hero Factor equation is: **Operational Excellence + Hero Intensity = Your Hero Factor.** To determine your scores, rate yourself on the following 25 statements as thoughtfully and honestly as you can. *Just be clear whether you're asking them about your organization or your leadership.* Don't mix up the two, and don't let your team do that, either.

While these questions are all written in the first-person plural:

> ▼ If you're asking about the organization, focus on the whole organization when it comes to its Operational Excellence and Hero Intensity.

> ▼ If you're asking about your leadership and you're not responsible for the whole organization, focus on the team or teams you're directly responsible for when it comes to Operational Excellence and on you as a leader when it comes to Hero Intensity.

When you're done, use the answer key to add up your scores (warning: math required) and determine your Operational Excellence and Hero Intensity. Then plot those scores on the Hero Factor Scale (see Figure 1.1 on page 12). You can also take the assessment for free online and have it scored for you by clicking the Hero Assessment link on the websites for The Hero Factor (https://HeroFactorBook.com), The Hero Club (https://heroceoclub.com/), or The Hayzlett Group (http://hayzlett.com/). Then take some time to reflect on your score and what you've read so far—or go back and read what you skipped and see how you can maintain, raise, and sustain your Hero Factor. Let's go!

OPERATIONAL EXCELLENCE

Answer these ten questions on a scale of 0 (Zero) to 10 (Hero). Use the following as a guide: Nope (0); Rarely (2.5); Kind Of (5); Yes, But We Could Do It Better (7.5); and Absolutely! (10).

1. Our business has real, consistent, and reliable results that are measurable and sustainable.

2. Our organization has seen success through tough times—small and big.

3. Our products and/or services exceed the competition and industry standards.

4. We have a broad, consistent set of customers/clients that we are connected to and always focus on serving and creating value for.

5. We have created external partnerships that provide expertise, reach, and knowledge beyond what we know.

6. We have reduced costs and increased efficiency, while still investing in equipment, systems, and people and their training.

7. Our workplace is productive and focused on growth in the short and long term.

8. We are willing to take risks and change and evolve our products, services, and leadership to meet workplace and marketplace demands.

9. We are constantly attracting and recruiting the best talent.

10. We have invested in and plan to add more value for the future through innovation, increased customer engagement, and new or improved products and services.

YOUR VALUES

Answer these ten questions on a scale of 0 (Zero) to 10 (Hero). Use the following as a guide: Nope (0); Rarely (2.5); Kind Of (5); Yes, But We Could Do It More (7.5); and Absolutely! (10).

1. Our values are clearly stated and prominently written out across the company for everyone to see.

2. Our people, leaders, and everyone we connect to can clearly state them back to us.

3. Our people live our values.

4. We review our values regularly, testing that they are being lived.

5. Our values have evolved.

6. We have shown the courage to stand up for the values we feel we cannot compromise.

7. We have shown the courage to test and reconsider our values when they are challenged and new thinking emerges.

VALUING OTHERS

Answer these ten questions on a scale of 0 (Zero) to 10 (Hero). Use the following as a guide: Nope (0); Rarely (2.5); Not As Much As We Want To (5); Yes, But We Could Be Better (7.5); and Absolutely! (10).

1. We value profits *and* people.

2. Our team and organization's culture doesn't just look strong; it feels strong and reflects our values.

3. We are inclusive of different perspectives *and* people.

4. We coach our people to be better—to lead, create, and have the independence to pursue opportunities others do not see.

5. Our organization and leaders . . .*

   a. See people as individuals and part of a team

   b. Care enough to listen

    c. Believe in alignment, not conformity, when it comes to goals

    d. Allow people to influence our direction

6. Our organization and leaders . . .*

    a. Are vulnerable

    b. Are transparent

    c. Are decisive

    d. Are calm through the chaos

7. We give back to our people in terms of sharing rewards and fair compensation, top to bottom.

8. We give more to our people and allow our people to do the same, top to bottom.

CALCULATE YOUR HERO FACTOR

Operational Excellence + Hero Intensity = Your Hero Factor

Your Operational Excellence Score

Add the scores from the ten Operational Excellence questions and divide by 10.

Your Hero Intensity Score

Add the scores from the seven questions in Your Values and the eight questions in Valuing Others and divide by 15.

* NOTE: For questions five and six in Valuing Others, add the four scores for letters a through d and divide by 4 before adding it to the others.

ACKNOWLEDGMENTS

To my family by blood and marriage and my work family at the C-Suite Network, Tallgrass, and Hayzlett, who are the real reasons for our success: I could not be prouder to stand by you and experience the great people you are and the successes you achieve every day. Never stop.

To the team at Entrepreneur Press who produced this book; and to the courageous business heroes I have met on my journey, look up to everyday, and who maintain their commitment to serving others, especially everyone who contributed on these pages: Booyah!

And to Jim Eber, my co-author: You have saved my "bacon" numerous times. There is not a word here, or in any of our best-sellers, that is not better because of you. Thank you, my brother.

ABOUT THE
AUTHOR

Jeffrey Hayzlett, founder of The Hayzlett Group, is a global business celebrity, prime-time TV and radio-show host, bestselling author, sought-after keynote speaker, and sometime cowboy.

Jeffrey is chairman of C-Suite Network, home of the world's most trusted network of C-Suite leaders, and host of *C-Suite With Jeffrey Hayzlett* and *Executive Perspectives* on C-Suite TV and the business podcast *All Business With Jeffrey Hayzlett* on C-Suite Radio. A well-traveled public speaker and former Fortune 100 CMO, Jeffrey is the author of three previous best-selling business books: *Think Big, Act Bigger: The Rewards of Being Relentless* (Entrepreneur Press, 2015); *Running the Gauntlet:*

Essential Business Lessons to Lead, Drive Change, and Grow Profits (McGraw-Hill, 2012); and *The Mirror Test: Is Your Business Really Breathing?* (Business Plus, 2011).

One of the most compelling figures in business today, Jeffrey has been inducted into five business halls of fame, including the National Speakers Association Hall of Fame, Sales & Marketing Executives International Academy of Achievement Sales & Marketing Hall of Fame, Business Marketing Association's Hall of Fame, and The College of Business Administration Direct Marketers Hall of Fame. He has also received numerous global awards and honors, including the Frost & Sullivan Lifetime Achievement Award for marketing and the Industry Award of Distinction from the National Association of Quick Printers.

As a leading business expert, Jeffrey is a frequent media guest and has shared his executive insight and commentary on Bloomberg, MSNBC, and Fox Business, as well as countless publications and radio shows. A turnaround architect of the highest order, a maverick marketer, and C-Suite executive who delivers scalable campaigns, Jeffrey embraces traditional modes of customer engagement and possesses a remarkable cachet of mentorship, corporate governance, and brand building. When he is not traveling the country in search of amazing bacon or enjoying a fine scotch in New York City, he lives in South Dakota with his family.

INDEX

Dear Reader,

Thanks for committing to *The Hero Factor* to the end and leading with tenacity and integrity. Now, I encourage you to take your commitment to the next level by pledging yourself to hero leadership and joining The Hero Club. Go to heroceoclub.com for your invitation.

The Hero Club is for CEOs and founders who have the vision and drive to take their companies to the next level; who want to be surrounded by and connected to other like-minded leaders, entrepreneurs, and investors; and who have all pledged to give back and more to their people, communities, and the next generation hero leaders.

Our purpose is to empower our members with relationships, resources, education, funding, and experiences to keep evolving and transforming their cultures and grow more. Through retreats and summits, we gain access to member-only education, problem solving, and proven business methodologies that help to ensure that our companies stay on the Hero path and are poised for faster and bigger success. We are also privileged to access the C-Suite Network platform that connects us with other entrepreneurs and C-Suite level decision-makers across North America.

I hope to see you at our next event.

Sincerely,

Jeffrey Hayzlett

CPSIA information can be obtained
at www.ICGtesting.com
Printed in the USA
BVHW040838180620
581802BV00008B/71

9 781642 011319